THE WORLDS OF
SHAKESPEARE

WILLIAM SHAKESPEARE

THE WORLDS OF
SHAKESPEARE

by Marchette Chute and Ernestine Perrie

DRAWINGS BY FREDERICK FRANCK

E. P. DUTTON & CO., Inc.
New York   1963

Published simultaneously in Canada by
Clarke, Irwin & Company Limited, Toronto and Vancouver

Library of Congress Catalog Card Number: 63-15779

INTRODUCTION I

by Marchette Chute

IT IS THE sign of a good playwright that he is able to draw his audience into the special world of his own imagination. Hedda Gabler belongs wholly to the world of Ibsen, the Duchess of Malfi to that of Webster, Miss Julie to Strindberg's, Mrs. Malaprop to Sheridan's. In each case, the audience enters willingly into the world that is created around these people, and it is in this world alone that they move and have their being.

The more completely each dramatist is able to create on the stage his own special view of reality and persuade his audience to share it, the less able he is to enter any other. This has been true of all the major playwrights of the world, from Aristophanes and Euripides to Molière and Racine. The great realists do not have the vision of poets; the men of comedy cannot write tragedy.

The one major dramatist of whom this is not true is William Shakespeare. There are thirty-six plays in the First Folio, and it might almost be said that there are thirty-six worlds. Shakespeare moves from lyric romance to realistic middle-class comedy, from soaring tragedy to earthbound buffoonery, to farce, to melodrama, to high comedy, and back to tragedy again; and he does all this with such apparently effortless ease that it is difficult to remember he is achieving what ought to be impossible. Shakespeare is not only capable of entering every human situation on every conceivable level but he is also capable of creating the whole of the special atmosphere that surrounds it. Rosalind, Lear, Bottom, and Macbeth exist in very different worlds. Yet Shakespeare can enter all of these worlds and persuade his audience to enter with him.

To understand the full force of this achievement, it would

be necessary to see all thirty-six plays acted, one after the other, on the stage. Since this is seldom possible, we offer *The Worlds of Shakespeare* as a kind of introduction. It is a distillation which cannot give the whole of Shakespeare's infinite variety but can at least suggest it.

Our first act is called "The World of Love" and presents six love scenes. There are many kinds of love in Shakespeare's plays, but these six are all on the subject of love between a man and a woman.

The tone of the first scene, from *Henry V,* is one of comic and courtly elegance, of a kind that no one but Shakespeare would have dared insert into a patriotic history play. It concerns the moment when King Henry, that magnificent and undefeated warrior, finds himself suddenly plunged into the unaccustomed role of lover. Moreover, he is trying to woo a lady who is princess of the land he has just conquered. Their scene together is one of the prettiest bits of rueful courtship ever presented on a stage, with the medieval convention of courtly love stood gracefully on its head.

The next scene, from *As You Like It,* belongs to the pastoral tradition. It has a sunlit tone that could only have been conceived in the best and most obliging of forests, but Orlando and Rosalind resemble no pastoral lovers that ever were before. They are too intelligent, and they take too real a delight in each other's company. Rosalind's helpful advice on the art of conducting a love affair is, in its less respectable moments, reminiscent of that given by Chaucer's Wife of Bath, but Rosalind possesses, in addition, the civilized gift of being able to laugh at herself.

The third scene, from *Richard III,* is purest melodrama. That evil hunchback whose name is Richard Plantagenet is determined to marry a woman whose husband he has murdered, and he gets his way in a crescendo of lies. Shakespeare, to get his own way with the audience, uses a stylized and almost hypnotic rhetoric that rises to an inevitable climax. In the world which Shakespeare has created for Richard and Anne, the special world of evil that knows its own dark laws,

Richard is as irresistible as his sword. He is also, to add a final glitter to the scene, a sardonic humorist who is highly amused by his own success.

The fourth scene is from *The Tempest* and turns to a world of perfect innocence. Miranda is that dream of the poets, the untouched virgin whom only one man can awaken, and she is as protected from reality on her father's enchanted island as any Sleeping Beauty in a thicket of thorns. Her speech has a child's simplicity and directness and she evokes the same response from Ferdinand, so that the young lovers are almost children together.

The fifth scene is from *Troilus and Cressida* and touches a bitter note that is sometimes, and mistakenly, called modern. The disillusioned weariness that can exist in any society is, in this case, the result of seven years of useless warfare. Cressida is the sort of woman who, in any period, will attach herself to the nearest man; but she is also a woman of Troy, that city of disenchantment, and she is tormented by a degree of self-knowledge that deprives her of the pleasure a more whole-hearted courtesan could achieve.

The final scene is the murder from *Othello,* one of the most terrifying intervals of sustained dialogue that Shakespeare ever achieved. This is a world wholly unlike any of the others, with self-torment and innocence and evil rising to a climax of human pain. Othello, the great general, has been led by Iago down the blind path of jealousy into the final act of murder. His words are born of an enormity of cruelty, anguish and love, while those of his young wife are as helpless as the wings of a bird beating against stone.

It is not difficult to understand how a great dramatist might be able to write such a scene. It is more difficult to see how the same man could also have written the other five, to say nothing of the hundreds of other scenes that owe their birth to him.

The second act of *The Worlds of Shakespeare* is called "The World of Music" and it attempts to suggest one of the ways in which Shakespeare was able to achieve so incredible a variety. Shakespeare was a very great poet, with an ear for words and a mastery over them which made it possible for him to create any mood he chose. If words are music, Shakespeare was the whole orchestra.

Our second act opens with the most obvious form of his music by evoking two of his songs. One is a green song of spring, ending with the light mockery of the cuckoo; the other is a white song of winter, ending with the cold call of the owl; and both are as accurate as a countryman could make them. They are from one of the earliest of Shakespeare's plays, *Love's Labour's Lost,* and are examples of the lyric gift that was apparently his from the first. His plays are laced with songs, the comedies especially; and some of the loveliest poems in the English language are scattered through them with the casual hand that could reach for any jewel it needed out of an inexhaustible treasury.

The second act of *The Worlds of Shakespeare* continues with three examples of pure word magic. There is the moonlit passage from *The Merchant of Venice* in which Lorenzo evokes for Jessica the beauty of a summer night in the softest of vowels and the most silvery of consonants. Then there is a leap to the trumpet-like call to arms from *Henry V,* so bright a persuasion to courage that centuries later, when Shakespeare's island was threatened with invasion, the English turned to it with a glad lifting of the heart. And lastly, there is the voodoo-like beat of a drum in the incantation of the witches from *Macbeth.*

This kind of music can easily be isolated from the plays, and perhaps it too often is. For the plays are plays, not collections of famous lines, and Shakespeare does not use his poetry as a form of display but as a force for illumination.

To illustrate this, our second act continues by pulling a single thread from *Macbeth*—the relationship between Macbeth and his wife that leads up to their act of murder. The subtle interaction of these two upon each other's emotions is built up as intricately as a musical score. Each phrase in the dialogue is poetry in itself; yet it is at the same time a characterization, a furthering of the plot, and an extraordinary evocation of natural and supernatural evil as it rises to its climax, the act of violence in the night whose blood darkens the rest of the play.

The man who could do this could also relax into pure nonsense, and for a few moments the second act relaxes with him. *A Midsummer Night's Dream* is touched with moonshine, and one of its most foolish and endearing episodes occurs when a group of amateur actors try to cast a play. In an earlier comedy Shakespeare had already presented anxious amateurs like these, but here there is an even more earnest idiocy of good intentions, especially in the case of Nick Bottom. Dear Bottom! He is the expert who always knows more about the show than the producer does and who could act the leading lady too if only someone would let him. He reappears in every generation, and Shakespeare has made him irresistible and immortal.

Then our second act turns again to Shakespeare as a writer of tragedy and once more pulls a single thread out of a play to show the extraordinary nature of the fabric. In this case the tragedy is *King Lear* and the thread is Lear's relationship to his three daughters. The basic human problem is a simple one, a story of unwanted old age that could be found on any city street, just as the narrative essentials of *Macbeth* might be found in any police record. But again the people and the story have been raised to the heights of great tragedy, with every movement of the mind made more intense by the infinite variations in the music.

Even in this brief indication of the story, the range and versatility of the language are as extraordinary as the uses to which it has been put. There is the grandiloquent formality of the old monarch when he is still on his throne and able to distribute land as largess, the stumbling rhythms of his gathering confusion and rage, the magnificent storm-like outburst that matches the elements, the broken movement of his madness, the drained and exhausted simplicity of his speech when he wakens in Cordelia's arms, the peaceful wisdom with which he welcomes their brief hours together, and the terrible, splintered cry of agony at the close. Quite apart from any other quality in this play, it is an almost unbelievable example of what the English language can do when it is under the control of a writer who is wholly its master.

Shakespeare could write tragedy on any level, and he could do the same with comedy. He even delighted in broad farce, and *The Worlds of Shakespeare* closes with the lively vigor of *The Taming of the Shrew*. Of all his plays, this one shows most clearly the *commedia dell'arte* tradition—the comedy of the craft—that was at the base of so much English theatre, but Shakespeare never permitted it to become merely a play of comic situation. The world of Petruchio and Katharina has its own kind of engaging humanity, and like each of Shakespeare's many worlds it is presented with the same sure stagecraft that makes it instantly communicable to a theatre audience.

To a greater degree than any other playwright in history, Shakespeare was a practical man of the theatre. He began his career as an actor before he became a playwright, and he continued to be an actor throughout the whole of his connection with the stage. He appeared in other men's plays as well as his own, so that Ben Jonson listed him as one of the "comedians" in *Every Man in his Humour* and as one of the "tragedians" in *Sejanus*. All day long, every day in the year, for some twenty years, Shakespeare lived in that strange, practical world of make-believe whose tools are human breath and the power of the audience's imagination. He was never separated for a moment from the craft of the theatre, from the techniques that create illusion, just as he was never separated from the audiences upon whose emotions, for twenty years, he so magically and successfully played.

Shakespeare entered the English theatre at a fortunate time for himself and the world, at a time when the actors were in control. Shakespeare and his associates were their own directors, producers, company managers, business managers, and even, after the joint profits of several successful years had made it possible, the owners of their own theatre building. They were directly responsible for everything that served to bring the play and the audience together, and Shakespeare never moved in a world of literary theory that was divorced from practical stagecraft. It was partly for this reason that he was not, in his own day, considered a great poet. He was considered a successful commercial playwright, one of several actors who wrote popular plays in their spare time. He was evidently content to have it so, for he turned the whole greatness of his vision and the glory of his poetry to the service of what was believed to be a contemptible medium—the stage.

Shakespeare was an actor, writing for actors, and he made no attempt to protect the words he had put on paper once they had lived their ephemeral life on the stage. Unlike Ben Jonson, he had no interest in seeing his plays in print. It was seven years after his death that two of his fellow actors, loving him and his work, managed to bring his plays into the protection of the First Folio; and it was everyone else in England, readers and playgoers, who took his words into the safety of their love from that time forward.

So it turned out that his words were not ephemeral. They are reborn every night in the voices of actors on stages all over the world, and nearly every country has the settled conviction that Shakespeare is somehow its own particular property. Any theatre can adjust to him, and generations of actors have proved that he never wrote a part which was not actable in the context of even the most alien nation. Ganapatrao played Hamlet in India for forty years, and Shakespeare's hero seemed as real to the people of India as he does to Russians or Germans.

Shakespeare's plays flourish everywhere, even when the words are no longer the English words he used and have undergone the approximation of a translation. Therefore, the two actors who speak his words in *The Worlds of Shakespeare* are not assigned to any period or any nation. They are merely HE and SHE, a man and woman who belong to Shakespeare's profession. They can be members of any race and dressed in the fashion of any century, for their purpose is merely to show a little of the vast universe of Shakespeare's art and the good fortune of the players who interpret it.

INTRODUCTION II

by Ernestine Perrie

As a child, I used to think William Shakespeare was an Italian. It seemed to me his plays were always set in Italian cities—Padua, Verona, Messina. His characters had Italian names—Petruchio, Romeo, Iago. I thought *Amleto* was Italian too and *Danimarca* was an Italian kingdom in a faraway time. Later on I found that *Danimarca* was Denmark and *Amleto* was Hamlet and *"essere o non essere"* was originally set down as "to be or not to be" by a genius who was English.

I had acquired my Shakespeare by osmosis, even before I could read, because I lived in a theatre where he was played in Italian. It was the Washington Square Theatre in North Beach, San Francisco, and I lived there with my family and ten other Italian actors. We did live there, truly—we only went home to sleep. The rest of the time they worked and I watched them. I thought them the most beautiful people in the world, with their resonant voices, exquisite manners, their canes and fur collars. They were more than beautiful; they were expert theatricians, and I never tired of listening to them.

My father headed the company. He had had the good fortune to come to this country as a boy of seventeen as a protégé of the great Eleonora Duse. While in New York he met and admired a young Italian actress who at fourteen was playing a character part in *Othello* while the leading man's wife, a lady of some years, was playing the heroine. My father made two vows: to cast the young actress in the proper parts, opposite himself, and to marry her. Both of which he did. For a time they toured the United States, playing Shakespeare to American audiences. The tour took them to San Francisco where they met other Italian actors who had arrived by other routes with other companies. The Italians of San Francisco were particularly alive and responsive. They supported their opera vociferously, they greeted visiting Italian companies with wild enthusiasm, and when they were offered Shakespeare they offered in return a fervent kind of listening. What actors could ask for more?

They met one night at the Fior d'Italia, a favorite Italian restaurant which is still there, and marked up a tablecloth with sums. Three items figured prominently: the cost of a lease on the Washington Square Theatre, the cost for show bills, and the expense of costumes. Very little was allotted to scenery and lighting since San Francisco Italians, whether they came from Fisherman's Wharf or Russian Hill, could be counted on for vivid imagination. When the total was drawn and the sum divided equally, each actor pledged to contribute his part toward a permanent theatre home of their own in which they would share profit or loss. A handshake and a glass of wine sealed the contract. On the same tablecloth was drawn a list of plays to include Pirandello as well as Sardou, Goldoni as well as Dumas, and *Blossom Time* as well as *Hamlet*. The Shakespeare leads would kick their heels in *Blossom Time* and love it; the musical comedy leads would play the bits in Shakespeare and glory in it. They were to be their own masters, settle down in one home and live the good theatre life—a life free of competition, pressure, fear of closings or critics' notices. They served as critic to each other; their strength was in their interdependence.

It was my privilege to watch it all happen. To be a child and to have a whole theatre for your world is to go through the looking glass a hundred times a day—what a frantic, joyous parade! Yet, even though it all rings in my ear, what I still hear most clearly is the deep silence of concentration during the Shakespeare rehearsals. On those days everything seemed to stop, or, I should say, everything seemed to begin.

The company called itself *La Moderna* (the modern one) but they were as ancient as *commedia dell'arte*. They all had the same heritage. They honored and respected it. They had passed it on for centuries because it was theatre wisdom. A farce was a farce, you gave it your laughter; a tragedy was a tragedy, you gave it your tears—never forgetting that in the essence of one was compounded the essence of the other. Above all, they knew that nothing was, except that which was communicated. Theirs was no peephole theatre. They made no pretense that the audience was not there; they never played for themselves but for their people. To them, they made an offering—the play, with all of themselves in it. To give all of themselves, they had to have a play that asked everything of them. The memorable nights at the Washington Square were the nights on which the *Moderna* played Shakespeare.

Changing conditions eventually ended the *Moderna*. Its members went their several ways and a number of the actors, including my parents, found their way into the American theatre. I did too, but not without an uneasy sense of alienation, a persistent searching for something that really had no reason to be there. The first day I reported to work in an American theatre, I looked around for the prompter's cue sheet which I expected to find hanging up backstage. Our theatre had never functioned without one. Every actor expected to consult it and check his entrances and his props by it. We called it a *"butta-fuori,"* which, literally translated, means a "throw-out." Some long-forgotten stage manager had named it that because it spared him the necessity of having to round up an actor backstage to "throw" him out onto the stage when his cue came. I had a special fondness for a *"butta-fuori"* because one of the first assignments my father had given me was to make one up. But it was not there where I expected it to be. I asked for it but was told, naturally, that there was no need for such a thing. I missed it for a long time.

I found it again years later, but I found it in the pages of a book: on page 166 of Marchette Chute's *Shakespeare of London*. "To make sure that all the properties were ready when they should be and that the actors would remember all their cues for entrances, a large sheet of paper was pasted on a board and hung on a peg at some conspicuous point backstage." It had hung backstage at the Globe Theatre as it had in the Washington Square. The more I read of that exhilarating account of Shakespeare's London, the more San Francisco seemed to turn into London and what I had thought too uniquely Italian was more nearly Elizabethan. The same fervent audiences, the same fervent players. The actors of the *Moderna* on their small scale, as those of the Globe on their history-making level, were using the same ways and means, were motivated by the same principles, animated by the same passion. Above all, they were guided by the same fundamental objective: ensemble playing of the highest order. The Italian language has a noun for it. It is *affiatamento*. When a company possesses it, that company has mastered the art of "breathing in unison."

One of the points we have tried to bring out in *The Worlds of Shakespeare* is the exhilaration actors can feel when they work together with nothing more than a plank, a passion, and a master to surrender themselves to. It is to them this book is dedicated.

NOTE

The Worlds of Shakespeare has been constructed out of selections from twelve of Shakespeare's plays, which have been adapted to the use of two actors. This has mostly been done by cutting but there have also been a few actual changes.

In Act I, three lines that originally belonged to Alice are given to the Princess Katherine and three lines that King Henry addresses to Alice are addressed to Katherine instead. One of Celia's and one of Orlando's lines have been given to Rosalind, and a line originally spoken by Pandarus has been given to Cressida.

In Act II, a line that originally belonged to Banquo has been given to Lady Macbeth and a line of Cornwall's has been given to Regan. In the section from *The Taming of the Shrew*, a line that Petruchio speaks at the end of the play has been substituted for a somewhat similar line that he speaks earlier.

Spelling and punctuation have been modernized throughout.

M.C. and E.P.

PROGRAM

ACT I

ACT II

THE WORLD OF
LOVE

ACT ONE

When the curtain rises the stage is dark, except for a central area which is faintly lit and seems to be floating in space. This gradually reveals itself as a raised platform, about six feet by eight, which has shallow steps leading up to it on all four sides.

In the center of the platform and slightly to the rear, there is a large open box. It has something of the look of a treasure chest and something of an actor's trunk.

A man and a woman are standing, in a tableau, on either side of the box. They are wearing costumes which belong to no particular period or country but which complement each other in line and color and are designed for easy movement. They each hold an object which they have obviously taken out of the box, SHE a mirror and HE a mask, and they are looking at them as if searching for an identity.

They stand motionless, as if suspended in time. As the light brightens, they stir.

HE: What is an actor?

SHE: Who is he?

HE: Every one?

SHE: No one?

HE: Always?

SHE: Never?

HE: Truly?

SHE: Falsely?

HE: Perhaps.

SHE: Perhaps not.

The light continues to brighten and they begin to lose their look of emptiness. They put the props they have been holding back into the box and close the lid, as if to free themselves. Then they begin to move down the steps and toward the empty forestage.

HE: Then that is to say, part of all and all of nothing—

SHE: It is to say, sometimes for all time and sometimes for a moment—

HE: Sometimes deeply, profoundly . . . sometimes not—

They have reached the bottom step and move toward the forestage as if to get closer to the audience. They speak tentatively, as if thinking aloud.

SHE: It is . . . to be a sail hanging useless until the wind gives it direction.

Her body responds to the image she has invoked.

HE: It is . . . to be a puppet that is motionless until the strings are touched.

SHE: If the wind is powerful and knows its course, then the sail unfolds to the sky, taut in its every fiber.

HE: That is what it's like to be an actor.

Their movements are now completely free.

SHE: To invite—

HE: To respond—

SHE: To list and turn to catch the fullest current.

HE: There are some currents so strong they nearly wrench the sail from the mast . . . like Lear.

SHE: Some so crossed they tear and shred . . . like Macbeth.

HE: There is the ripple of laughter, the stillness of innocence—

SHE: The fury of tears—

HE: He has given us everything.

SHE: More lives than one life can contain.

HE: More worlds than one world can encompass.

SHE: No one has ever asked more of us, and so we honor him.

There is a pause.

HE: Take love, for instance.

SHE: Between men and women.

HE: A fascinating subject.

SHE: Indeed.

HE: Agreed.

SHE: Every playwright in the world has something to say about it.

HE: And we have played many lovers.

SHE: Of one kind and then of another.

HE: But never so many as he has conceived.

SHE: Never have we moved so far as he has taken us.

HE: May we take you?

HE *makes a stylized gesture of the arms and hands as though he were finger-painting in the air.*

HE: A wash of shadows here.

The lights of the forestage dim obediently. Then HE *turns his back to the audience and makes a sweeping movement in the air, as if he were gathering the light into his hands and focusing it on the platform.*

HE: And a play of light here.

The platform lights up.

SHE: Well done!

They return to the platform, which is now brightly lit and ready for playing. HE *opens the closed box.*

HE: We will need our trunk. No actor travels without one. *(In a practical tone of voice.)* It's a tool chest.

SHE: It's a treasure chest.

HE (*remembering what he has forgotten*): It is a treasure chest.
(*He reaches in and takes out a nosegay of blue flowers.*)
A bouquet for you.

SHE (*also reaching into the box*): And a crown for you.

HE *stands holding the bright object in his hands, and his eyes
sweep over the platform. This is to be their playing area, the
center and focus of each of their scenes, and he lights up in
excitement at the prospect.*

HE (*moving down a step so that he can address the audience*):
It is given to me to be a king—King Henry of England.
He is a warrior who has fought many mighty battles, and
now he has conquered France.

SHE (*sharing his excitement*): It is given to me to be a princess of France, and I find that King Henry wants to marry
me. It is true that he has just conquered my country and
yet somehow I find him appealing. I do not really know
his language—

HE: And I know hers even less.

SHE: So we find ourselves involved in a kind of duel—a very
lighthearted and courtly one—

HE: Which I win.

SHE (*smiling at him*): Yes.

HE (*turning to the audience and speaking formally*): The pro-
posal scene from HENRY THE FIFTH.

*They turn their backs to the audience and stand for a mo-
ment relaxed and still. Then they begin to gather themselves
up.* HE *puts the crown on his head and* SHE *arranges her nose-*

gay demurely. There is a flourish of trumpets and they turn back to the audience in character as King Henry of England and Princess Katherine of France.

HENRY

Fair Katherine, and most fair,
Will you vouchsafe to teach a soldier terms,
Such as will enter at a lady's ear
And plead his love-suit to her gentle heart?

KATHERINE

Your Majesty sall mock at me. I cannot speak your England.

HENRY

O fair Katherine, if you will love me soundly with your French heart, I will be glad to hear you confess it brokenly with your English tongue. Do you like me, Kate?

KATHERINE

Pardonnez-moi, I cannot tell vat is 'like me.'

HENRY

An angel is like you, Kate, and you are like an angel.

KATHERINE

O bon Dieu! les langues des hommes sont pleines de tromperies.

HENRY

What say you, fair one? that the tongues of men are full of deceits?

KATHERINE

Oui.

HENRY

I'faith, Kate, my wooing is fit for thy understanding.
I am glad thou canst speak no better English; for if
thou couldst, thou wouldst find me such a plain king
that thou wouldst think I had sold my farm to buy
my crown. I know no ways to mince it in love, but
directly to say, 'I love you.' Then, if you urge me
farther than to say, 'Do you in faith?' I wear out my
suit. Give me your answer, i'faith do, and so clap
hands and a bargain. How say you, lady?

KATHERINE

Sauf votre honneur, me understand vell.

HENRY

Marry, if you would put me to verses or to dance for
your sake, Kate, why you undid me. For the one, I
have neither words nor measure; and for the other,
I have no strength in measure, yet a reasonable measure in strength. If I could win a lady at leapfrog, or
by vaulting into my saddle with my armor on my
back, under the correction of bragging be it spoken,
I should quickly leap into a wife. Or if I might buffet
for my love, or bound my horse for her favors, I
could lay on like a butcher and sit like a jackanapes,
never off. But, before God, Kate, I cannot look
greenly nor gasp out my eloquence, nor I have no
cunning in protestation; only downright oaths, which
I never use till urged, nor never break for urging.
If thou canst love a fellow of this temper, Kate, whose
face is not worth sunburning, that never looks in his
glass for love of anything he sees there, let thine eye
be thy cook. I speak to thee plain soldier. If thou
canst love me for this, take me; if not, to say to thee
that I shall die, is true; but for thy love, by the Lord,
no; yet I love thee too. And while thou liv'st, dear
Kate, take a fellow of plain and uncoined constancy;

for he perforce must do thee right, because he hath
not the gift to woo in other places. For these fellows
of infinite tongue, that can rhyme themselves into
ladies' favors, they do always reason themselves out
again. What! A speaker is but a prater, a rhyme is
but a ballad. A good leg will fall, a straight back will
stoop, a black beard will turn white, a curled pate
will grow bald, a fair face will wither, a full eye will
wax hollow; but a good heart, Kate, is the sun and
the moon, or rather the sun and not the moon; for it
shines bright and never changes, but keeps his course
truly. If thou would have such a one, take me; and
take me, take a soldier; take a soldier, take a king.
And what sayst thou then to my love? Speak, my
fair, and fairly, I pray thee.

KATHERINE

Is it possible dat I sould love de enemy of France?

HENRY

No, it is not possible you should love the enemy of
France, Kate; but, in loving me, you should love the
friend of France; for I love France so well that I will
not part with a village of it; I will have it all mine.
And, Kate, when France is mine and I am yours, then
yours is France and you are mine.

KATHERINE

I cannot tell vat is dat.

HENRY

No, Kate? I will tell thee in French, which I am sure
will hang upon my tongue like a new-married wife
about her husband's neck, hardly to be shook off. Je
quand sur le possession de France, et quand vous avez
le possession de moi—let me see, what then? Saint
Denis be my speed!—donc votre est France et vous

êtes mienne. It is as easy for me, Kate, to conquer the kingdom as to speak so much more French. I shall never move thee in French, unless it be to laugh at me.

KATHERINE

Sauf votre honneur, le Français que vous parlez, il est meilleur que l'Anglais lequel je parle.

HENRY

No, faith, is't not, Kate. But thy speaking of my tongue, and I thine, most truly-falsely, must needs be granted to be much at one. But, Kate, dost thou understand thus much English? Canst thou love me?

KATHERINE

I cannot tell.

HENRY

Good Kate, mock me mercifully, the rather, gentle Princess, because I love thee cruelly. If ever thou beest mine, Kate, as I have a saving faith within me tells me thou shalt, I get thee with scambling, and thou must therefore needs prove a good soldier-breeder. Shall not thou and I, between Saint Denis and Saint George, compound a boy, half French, half English, that shall go to Constantinople and take the Turk by the beard? Shall we not? What sayst thou, my fair flower-de-luce?

KATHERINE

I do not know dat.

HENRY

No; 'tis hereafter to know, but now to promise. Do but now promise, Kate, you will endeavor for your French part of such a boy; and for my English moiety,

HENRY AND KATHERINE

take the word of a king and a bachelor. How answer
you, la plus belle Katherine du monde, mon très cher
et divin déesse?

KATHERINE

Your Majestee ave fausse French enough to deceive
de most sage demoiselle dat is en France.

HENRY

Now, fie upon my false French! By mine honor, in
true English, I love thee, Kate; by which honor I
dare not swear thou lovest me; yet my blood begins
to flatter me that thou dost, notwithstanding the poor
and untempering effect of my visage. Now beshrew
my father's ambition! He was thinking of civil wars
when he got me. Therefore was I created with a stub-
born outside, with an aspect of iron, that, when I
come to woo ladies, I fright them. But, in faith, Kate,
the elder I wax, the better I shall appear. My comfort is that old age, that ill layer up of beauty, can
do no more spoil upon my face. Thou hast me, if thou
hast me, at the worst; and thou shalt wear me, if thou
wear me, better and better. And therefore tell me,
most fair Katherine, will you have me? Put off your
maiden blushes, avouch the thoughts of your heart
with the looks of an empress, take me by the hand,
and say 'Harry of England, I am thine': which word
thou shalt no sooner bless mine ear withal, but I will
tell thee aloud 'England is thine, France is thine, and
Henry Plantagenet is thine.' Come, your answer in
broken music; for thy voice is music, and thy English
broken; therefore, queen of all, Katherine, break thy
mind to me in broken English; wilt thou have me?

KATHERINE

Dat is as it sall please de roi mon père.

HENRY

Nay, it will please him well, Kate; it shall please him, Kate.

KATHERINE

Den it sall also content me.

HENRY

Upon that I kiss your hand, and I call you my queen.

KATHERINE

Laissez, mon seigneur, laissez, laissez! Ma foi, je ne veux point que vous abaissiez votre grandeur en baisant la main d'une votre seigneurie indigne servi-teur. Excusez-moi, je vous supplie, mon très-puissant seigneur.

HENRY

Then I will kiss your lips, Kate.

KATHERINE

Les dames et demoiselles pour être baisées devant leur noces, il n'est pas la coutume de France.

HENRY

What say you?

KATHERINE

Dat it is not be de fashion pour les ladies of France —I cannot tell vat is 'baiser' en Anglish.

HENRY

To kiss.

KATHERINE

Your Majestee entendre bettre que moi.

HENRY

It is not a fashion for the maids in France to kiss before they are married, would you say?

KATHERINE

Oui, vraiment.

HENRY

O Kate, nice customs curtsy to great kings. Dear Kate, you and I cannot be confined within the weak list of a country's fashion. We are the makers of manners, Kate; and the liberty that follows our places stops the mouth of all find-faults, as I will do yours for upholding the nice fashion of your country in denying me a kiss. Therefore patiently, and yielding. *(Kissing her.)* You have witchcraft in your lips, Kate. There is more eloquence in a sugar touch of them than in the tongues of the French council; and they should sooner persuade Harry of England than a general petition of monarchs.

The King takes the hand of the Princess ceremoniously in his. They turn and leave the platform by the rear steps, the lights dimming as they go. The lights of the forestage go up.

HE *and* SHE *return around the base of the platform, one from each side, and meet in the center front. He is now holding the crown in his hand.*

SHE: And now, I think we should do a love scene in which the woman is in control. *(Virtuously.)* I feel we should strive for variety.

SHE *hands him her bouquet, and* HE *takes it and the crown back to the platform. He replaces these props in the box, taking out instead a scroll and a spray of green leaves.*

SHE: We will do a scene that is as gay and green as an emerald or as the leaves in the Forest of Arden. Here love is not a duel but a game—

HE *(returning)*: And one in which the lady makes up the rules as she goes along.

SHE *(placidly)*: Very good ones too.

HE: I am Orlando.

SHE: And I am Rosalind.

They start speaking together.

HE: Orlando and Rosalind fell in love—

SHE: Rosalind and Orlando fell in love—

They break off and smile, without losing the beat.

SHE: At—

HE: —first—

SHE: —sight.

HE *(explaining things to the audience)*: I only saw Rosalind once. Then I was driven away from my home and found refuge in the Forest of Arden, where I have been wandering about, writing poems to my beloved.

SHE: I was driven from home too, and so I disguised myself as a boy.

SHE *unhooks her skirt and hands it to him; she is now wearing tights.* HE *folds the skirt tidily, puts it in the box, and takes out a forester's cap of bright green. He sets it on her head, and she uses him as a kind of mirror to get it at the right angle.*

SHE: When I meet Orlando again, in the Forest of Arden, he naturally thinks I am a boy. It is a situation that no one could expect me to resist.

HE *(formally, to the audience)*: The encounter between Rosalind and Orlando in AS YOU LIKE IT.

As before, they turn their backs for a moment to the audience. There is the sound of a bird call and they turn back again, in character.

ORLANDO

Where dwell you, pretty youth?

ROSALIND

Here in the skirts of the forest, like fringe upon a petticoat.

ORLANDO

Your accent is something finer than you could purchase in so removed a dwelling.

ROSALIND

I have been told so of many; but indeed an old religious uncle of mine taught me to speak, who was in his youth an inland man; one that knew courtship too well, for there he fell in love. I have heard him read many lectures against it, and I thank God I am not a woman, to be touched with so many giddy offenses as he hath generally taxed their whole sex withal.

ORLANDO

Can you remember any of the principal evils that he laid to the charge of women?

ROSALIND

There were none principal; they were all like one another as half-pence are, every one fault seeming monstrous till his fellow-fault came to match it.

ORLANDO

I prithee, recount some of them.

ROSALIND

No, I will not cast away my physic but on those that are sick. There is a man haunts the forest, that abuses our young plants with carving Rosalind on their barks; hangs odes upon hawthorns and elegies on brambles; all, forsooth, deifying the name of Rosalind. If I could meet that fancy-monger, I would give him some good counsel, for he seems to have the quotidian of love upon him.

ORLANDO

I am he that is so love-shaked; I pray you, tell me your remedy.

ROSALIND

There is none of my uncle's marks upon you: he taught me how to know a man in love, in which cage of rushes I am sure you are not prisoner.

ORLANDO

What were his marks?

ROSALIND

A lean cheek, which you have not; a blue eye and sunken, which you have not; a beard neglected, which you have not. Then your hose should be ungartered, your bonnet unbanded, your sleeve unbuttoned, your shoe untied and every thing about you demonstrating a careless desolation. But you are no such man; you are rather point-device in your accouterments, as loving yourself than seeming the lover of any other.

ORLANDO

Fair youth, I would I could make thee believe I love.

ROSALIND

Me believe it? You may as soon make her that you love believe it; which, I warrant, she is apter to do than to confess she does: that is one of the points in which women still give the lie to their consciences. But, in good sooth, are you he that hangs the verses on the trees, wherein Rosalind is so admired?

ORLANDO

I swear to thee, youth, by the white hand of Rosalind, I am that he, that unfortunate he.

ROSALIND

But are you so much in love as your rhymes speak?

ORLANDO

Neither rhyme nor reason can express how much.

ROSALIND

Love is merely a madness; and, I tell you, deserves as well a dark house and a whip as madmen do: and the reason why they are not so punished and cured is, that the lunacy is so ordinary that the whippers are in love too. Yet I profess curing it by counsel.

ORLANDO

Did you ever cure any so?

ORLANDO AND ROSALIND

ROSALIND

Yes, one, and in this manner. He was to imagine me his love, his mistress; and I set him every day to woo me: at which time would I, being but a moonish youth, grieve, be effeminate, changeable, longing and liking; proud, fantastical, apish, shallow, inconstant, full of tears, full of smiles; for every passion something and for no passion truly any thing, as boys and women are for the most part cattle of this color: would now like him, now loathe him; then entertain him, then forswear him; now weep for him, then spit at him; that I drave my suitor from his mad humor of love to a living humor of madness; which was, to forswear the full stream of the world and to live in a nook merely monastic. And thus I cured him; and this way will I take upon me to wash your liver as clean as a sound sheep's heart, that there shall not be one spot of love in't.

ORLANDO

I would not be cured, youth.

ROSALIND

I would cure you, if you would but call me Rosalind and woo me.

ORLANDO

Now, by the faith of my love, I will, good youth.

ROSALIND

Nay, you must call me Rosalind.

ORLANDO

Good-day and happiness, dear Rosalind!

ROSALIND

Why, how now, Orlando! where have you been all

this while? You a lover! And you serve me such another trick, never come in my sight more.

ORLANDO

My fair Rosalind, I come within an hour of my
promise.

ROSALIND

Break an hour's promise in love! He that will divide
a minute into a thousand parts, and break but a part
of the thousandth part of a minute in the affairs of
love, it may be said of him that Cupid hath clapped
him o' the shoulder, but I'll warrant him heart-whole.

ORLANDO

Pardon me, dear Rosalind.

ROSALIND

Come, woo me, woo me; for now I am in a holiday
humor and like enough to consent. What would you
say to me now, and I were your very, very Rosalind?

ORLANDO

I would kiss before I spoke.

ROSALIND

Nay, you were better speak first; and when you were
graveled for lack of matter, you might take occasion
to kiss. Very good orators, when they are out, they
will spit; and for lovers lacking—God warn us!—
matter, the cleanliest shift is to kiss.

ORLANDO

How if the kiss be denied?

ROSALIND

Then she puts you to entreaty, and there begins new
matter.

ORLANDO

Who could be out, being before his beloved mistress?

ROSALIND

Marry, that should you, if I were your mistress. Am
not I your Rosalind?

ORLANDO

I take some joy to say you are, because I would be
talking of her.

ROSALIND

Well, in her person, I say I will not have you.

ORLANDO

Then, in mine own person, I die.

ROSALIND

No, faith, die by attorney. The poor world is almost
six thousand years old, and in all this time there was
not any man died in his own person, videlicet, in a
love-cause. Troilus had his brains dashed out with a
Grecian club; yet he did what he could to die before,
and he is one of the patterns of love. Leander, he
would have lived many a fair year, though Hero had
turned nun, if it had not been for a hot midsummer
night; for, good youth, he went but forth to wash him
in the Hellespont and being taken with the cramp
was drowned: and the foolish chroniclers of that age
found it was 'Hero of Sestos.' But these are all lies:
men have died from time to time and worms have
eaten them, but not for love.

ORLANDO

I would not have my right Rosalind of this mind; for,
I protest, her frown might kill me.

ROSALIND

By this hand, it will not kill a fly. But come, now I
will be your Rosalind in a more coming-on disposi-
tion, and ask me what you will, I will grant it.

ORLANDO

Then love me, Rosalind.

ROSALIND

Yes, faith, will I, Fridays and Saturdays and all.

ORLANDO

And wilt thou have me?

ROSALIND

Aye, and twenty such.

ORLANDO

What sayest thou?

ROSALIND

Are you not good?

ORLANDO

I hope so.

ROSALIND

Why then, can one desire too much of a good thing?
Pray thee, marry me. (*Acting the part of a priest.*)
Will you, Orlando, have to wife this Rosalind?

ORLANDO

I will.

ROSALIND

Aye, but when?

ORLANDO

Why, now.

ROSALIND

Then you must say, 'I take thee, Rosalind, for wife.'

ORLANDO

I take thee, Rosalind, for wife.

ROSALIND

I might ask you for your commission; but I do take thee, Orlando, for my husband. There's a girl goes before the priest, and certainly a woman's thought runs before her actions.

ORLANDO

So do all thoughts; they are winged.

ROSALIND

Now tell me how long you would have her after you have possessed her.

ORLANDO

For ever and a day.

ROSALIND

Say 'a day' without the 'ever.' No, no, Orlando; men are April when they woo, December when they wed: maids are May when they are maids, but the sky changes when they are wives. I will be more jealous of thee than a Barbary cock-pigeon over his hen, more clamorous than a parrot against rain, more new-fangled than an ape, more giddy in my desires than a monkey: I will weep for nothing, like Diana in the fountain, and I will do that when you are disposed to be merry; I will laugh like a hyen, and that when thou art inclined to sleep.

ORLANDO

But will my Rosalind do so?

ROSALIND

By my life, she will do as I do.

ORLANDO

O, but she is wise.

ROSALIND

Or else she could not have the wit to do this: the
wiser the waywarder: make the doors upon a woman's
wit and it will out at the casement; shut that and
'twill out at the key-hole; stop that, 'twill fly with the
smoke out at the chimney.

ORLANDO

A man that had a wife with such a wit, he might say,
'Wit, whither wilt?'

ROSALIND

Nay, you might keep that check for it, till you met
your wife's wit going to your neighbor's bed.

ORLANDO

And what wit could wit have to excuse that?

ROSALIND

Marry, to say she came to seek you there. You shall
never take her without her answer, unless you take
her without her tongue. O, that woman that cannot
make her fault her husband's occasion, let her never
nurse her child herself, for she will breed it like a
fool!

ORLANDO

For these two hours, Rosalind, I will leave you.

ROSALIND

Alas, dear love, I cannot lack thee two hours!

ORLANDO

I must attend the Duke at dinner: by two o'clock I
will be with thee again.

ROSALIND

Aye, go your ways, go your ways; I knew what you
would prove: my friends told me as much, and I
thought no less: that flattering tongue of yours won
me: 'tis but one cast away, and so, come, death! Two
o'clock is your hour?

ORLANDO

Aye, sweet Rosalind.

ROSALIND

By my troth, and in good earnest, and so God mend
me, and by all pretty oaths that are not dangerous,
if you break one jot of your promise or come one
minute behind your hour, I will think you the most
pathetical break-promise, and the most hollow lover,
and the most unworthy of her you call Rosalind, that
may be chosen out of the gross band of the unfaithful: therefore beware my censure and keep your
promise.

ORLANDO

With no less religion than if thou wert indeed my
Rosalind: so adieu.

ROSALIND

Well, Time is the old justice that examines all such
offenders, and let Time try: adieu. (Exit Orlando.)
O, that thou didst know how many fathom deep I
am in love! But it cannot be sounded: my affection

hath an unknown bottom, like the Bay of Portugal.
I cannot be out of the sight of Orlando. I'll go find a
shadow and sigh till he come.

*During Rosalind's final lines, Orlando stands motionless in
the shadows, his face averted. When she finishes speaking the
lights on the platform dim, and the forestage lights up instead
as they return to it.*

SHE *collects the leaves and scroll and returns to the darkened
platform. When she comes back to the lighted forestage she is
wearing her skirt again and holding a veil and a sword.*

HE *(to the audience)*: That was a sunlit world in which love
was a friend. Now we move to another world entirely,
one that is monstrous with blood and intrigue and as
darkly magnificent as a ruby.

SHE *hands him the sword, and the light catches the red stone
in its hilt. Then she turns to the audience with the veil in her
hands.*

SHE: This is the mourning veil of the Lady Anne. She married
the son of Henry of Lancaster, King of England, and both
her husband and his father have been murdered.

HE: And this is the sword of their murderer, Richard Plantagenet the hunchback.

SHE: She knows he is the murderer.

HE: And yet he believes he can persuade her to marry him.
He does not lust after her. He lusts after the throne of
England, and her rank will help him to get it.

SHE: This is the day of the King's funeral, and Lady Anne
walks in the procession that carries his coffin.

They return to the now-lighted platform and lift a black cloth out of the box, each taking one end. It billows out as they open it and falls in a kind of pall over the box, covering it. HE *motions her away from the platform and addresses the audience.*

HE: The funeral procession will come from there. *(He indicates part of the forestage with a sweep of his hand.)* And it will pass here, by the church. Anne will not see her enemy at first, for he has hidden himself in the shadows. *(Formally.)* We give you the seduction scene from RICHARD THE THIRD.

They turn their backs to the audience. HE *buckles on the sword;* SHE *puts the veil over her head. Then she bows her head and stiffens into the rigidity of grief, and he writhes into the contorted posture of a hunchback. There is a sound of churchbells and of faint chanting, and they turn back to the audience as Richard and Anne. She moves slowly, as though in a procession, up to the box with the black drapery.*

ANNE

Set down, set down your honorable load,
If honor may be shrouded in a hearse,
Whilst I awhile obsequiously lament
The untimely fall of virtuous Lancaster.
Thou bloodless remnant of that royal blood,
Be it lawful that I invocate thy ghost,
To hear the lamentations of poor Anne,
Wife to thy Edward, to thy slaughtered son,
Stabbed by the selfsame hand that made these
       wounds.
Lo, in these windows that let forth thy life,
I pour the helpless balm of my poor eyes.
Come now towards Chertsey with your holy load.

RICHARD

Stay, you that bear the corse, and set it down.

ANNE

What black magician conjures up this fiend,
To stop devoted charitable deeds?
Avaunt, thou dreadful minister of hell!
Thou hadst but power over his mortal body,
His soul thou canst not have. Therefore be gone.

RICHARD

Sweet saint, for charity, be not so curst.

ANNE

Foul devil, for God's sake hence, and trouble us not;
For thou hast made the happy earth thy hell,
Filled it with cursing cries and deep exclaims.
If thou delight to view thy heinous deeds,
Behold this pattern of thy butcheries.
O God, which this blood mad'st, revenge his death!
O earth, which this blood drink'st, revenge his death!
Either heaven, with lightning, strike the murderer
    dead,
Or earth, gape open wide and eat him quick,
As thou dost swallow up this good king's blood,
Which his hell-governed arm hath butcherèd!

RICHARD

Lady, you know no rules of charity,
Which renders good for bad, blessings for curses.

ANNE

Villain, thou know'st no law of God nor man:
No beast so fierce but knows some touch of pity.

RICHARD

But I know none, and therefore am no beast.

ANNE

O wonderful, when devils tell the truth!

RICHARD

More wonderful, when angels are so angry.
Vouchsafe, divine perfection of a woman,
Of these supposèd crimes to give me leave,
By circumstance, but to acquit myself.

ANNE

Vouchsafe, diffused infection of a man,
For these known evils but to give me leave,
By circumstance, to curse thy cursèd self.

RICHARD

Fairer than tongue can name thee, let me have
Some patient leisure to excuse myself.

ANNE

Fouler than heart can think thee, thou canst make
No excuse current but to hang thyself.

RICHARD

By such despair I should accuse myself.

ANNE

And by despairing shalt thou stand excused,
For doing worthy vengeance on thyself,
That didst unworthy slaughter upon others.

RICHARD

Say that I slew them not.

ANNE

                    Why then they are not dead;
But dead they are, and, devilish slave, by thee.

RICHARD

I did not kill your husband.

ANNE

                              Why then he is alive.

RICHARD

Nay, he is dead, and slain by Edward's hand.

ANNE

In thy foul throat thou liest. Queen Margaret saw
Thy murderous falchion smoking in his blood,
The which thou once didst bend against her breast,
But that thy brothers beat aside the point.

RICHARD

I was provokèd by her slanderous tongue,
That laid their guilt upon my guiltless shoulders.

ANNE

Thou wast provokèd by thy bloody mind,
That never dreamt on aught but butcheries.
Didst thou not kill this king?

RICHARD

                              I grant ye.

ANNE

Dost grant me, hedgehog? then, God grant me too
Thou mayst be damnèd for that wicked deed!
Oh, he was gentle, mild, and virtuous.

RICHARD

The better for the King of heaven, that hath him.

ANNE

He is in heaven, where thou shalt never come.

RICHARD

Let him thank me, that holp to send him thither,
For he was fitter for that place than earth.

ANNE

And thou unfit for any place but hell.

RICHARD

Yes, one place else, if you will hear me name it.

ANNE

Some dungeon.

RICHARD

Your bed-chamber.

ANNE

Ill rest betide the chamber where thou liest!

RICHARD

So will it, madam, till I lie with you.

ANNE

I hope so.

RICHARD

I know so. But, gentle Lady Anne,
To leave this keen encounter of our wits,
And fall somewhat into a slower method,
Is not the causer of the timeless deaths
Of these Plantagenets, Henry and Edward,
As blameful as the executioner?

ANNE

Thou wast the cause, and most accursed effect.

RICHARD

Your beauty was the cause of that effect,
Your beauty, that did haunt me in my sleep

To undertake the death of all the world,
So I might live one hour in your sweet bosom.

ANNE

If I thought that, I tell thee, homicide,
These nails should rend that beauty from my cheeks.

RICHARD

These eyes could not endure that beauty's wreck;
You should not blemish it, if I stood by.
As all the world is cheerèd by the sun,
So I by that. It is my day, my life.

ANNE

Black night o'ershade thy day, and death thy life!

RICHARD

Curse not thyself, fair creature; thou art both.

ANNE

I would I were, to be revenged on thee.

RICHARD

It is a quarrel most unnatural,
To be revenged on him that loveth thee.

ANNE

It is a quarrel just and reasonable,
To be revenged on him that slew my husband.

RICHARD

He that bereft thee, lady, of thy husband,
Did it to help thee to a better husband.

ANNE

His better doth not breathe upon the earth.

RICHARD

He lives that loves thee better than he could.

ANNE

Name him.

RICHARD

Plantagenet.

ANNE

Why, that was he.

RICHARD

The selfsame name, but one of better nature.

ANNE

Where is he?

RICHARD

Here. —Why dost thou spit at me?

ANNE

Would it were mortal poison, for thy sake!

RICHARD

Never came poison from so sweet a place.

ANNE

Never hung poison on a fouler toad.
Out of my sight! thou dost infect mine eyes.

RICHARD

Thine eyes, sweet lady, have infected mine.
Those eyes of thine from mine have drawn salt tears,
Shamed their aspect with store of childish drops:
These eyes, which never shed remorseful tear,
Not when thy warlike father, like a child,

RICHARD AND ANNE

Told the sad story of my father's death,
And twenty times made pause to sob and weep,
That all the standers-by had wet their cheeks,
Like trees bedashed with rain. In that sad time
My manly eyes did scorn an humble tear;
And what these sorrows could not thence exhale,
Thy beauty hath, and made them blind with weeping.
I never sued to friend nor enemy,
My tongue could never learn sweet smoothing word;
But now thy beauty is proposed my fee,
My proud heart sues, and prompts my tongue to
    speak.
Teach not thy lip such scorn; for it was made
For kissing, lady, not for such contempt.
If thy revengeful heart cannot forgive,
Lo, here I lend thee this sharp-pointed sword,
Which if thou please to hide in this true breast,
And let the soul forth that adoreth thee,
I lay it naked to the deadly stroke,
And humbly beg the death upon my knee.
Nay, do not pause; for I did kill King Henry,
But 'twas thy beauty that provokèd me.
Nay, now dispatch; 'twas I that stabbed young
    Edward,
But 'twas thy heavenly face that set me on.
Take up the sword again, or take up me.

ANNE

Arise, dissembler: though I wish thy death,
I will not be thy executioner.

RICHARD

Then bid me kill myself, and I will do it.

ANNE

I have already.

RICHARD

That was in thy rage.
Speak it again, and even with the word,
This hand, which for thy love did kill thy love,
Shall for thy love kill a far truer love;
To both their deaths shalt thou be accessary.

ANNE

I would I knew thy heart.

RICHARD

'Tis figured in my tongue.

ANNE

I fear me both are false.

RICHARD

Then never was man true.

ANNE

Well, well, put up your sword.

RICHARD

Say then my peace is made.

ANNE

That shall you know hereafter.

RICHARD

But shall I live in hope?

ANNE

All men, I hope, live so.

RICHARD

Vouchsafe to wear this ring.

ANNE

To take is not to give.

RICHARD

Look how my ring encompasseth thy finger,
Even so thy breast encloseth my poor heart;
Wear both of them, for both of them are thine.
Bid me farewell.

ANNE

                'Tis more than you deserve;
But since you teach me how to flatter you,
Imagine I have said farewell already.   (She exits.)

RICHARD

Was ever woman in this humor wooed?
Was ever woman in this humor won?
I'll have her, but I will not keep her long.
What! I, that killed her husband and his father,
To take her in her heart's extremest hate,
With curses in her mouth, tears in her eyes,
The bleeding witness of my hatred by,
Having God, her conscience, and these bars against
     me,
And I no friends to back my suit withal,
But the plain devil and dissembling looks,
And yet to win her,—all the world to nothing!
Ha!
I do mistake my person all this while.
Upon my life, she finds, although I cannot,
Myself to be a marvelous proper man.
I'll be at charges for a looking-glass,
And entertain a score or two of tailors,
To study fashions to adorn my body.
Since I am crept in favor with myself,
I will maintain it with some little cost.
But first, I'll turn yon fellow in his grave,

And then return lamenting to my love.
Shine out, fair sun, till I have bought a glass,
That I may see my shadow as I pass.

*During Richard's soliloquy Anne remains motionless in the
shadows, her face averted. They return to the forestage when
the scene is over.*

HE *returns to the platform to put away the veil and sword
and to take out a heavy silver chain set with pearls.*

SHE: And now we will show you another aspect of love. This
is the springtime of youth and innocence, in a scene that
is as gentle and luminous as a pearl.

HE *(settling the chain around his shoulders)*: I, Ferdinand,
prince of Naples, have been shipwrecked on a magic island.

SHE: And I, Miranda, daughter of the lord of the island, have
been living here alone with my father. I never saw a
young man before.

HE *(complacently)*: Never.

SHE *(smiling)*: Which is, of course, somewhat to his advantage.

HE: I have seen many ladies, but none so lovely as Miranda.
I showed my admiration a little too clearly, and her father
has set me to piling logs.

SHE: And I have stolen out to watch him.

HE *(to the audience, formally)*: The love scene from THE
TEMPEST.

They turn their backs to the audience. There is the faint sound of water lapping on rocks, and they turn back as Ferdinand and Miranda. Ferdinand goes to lift an imaginary log and carry it to the platform, while Miranda watches, full of sympathy for his task and admiration for his prowess. The logs clearly become heavier when he realizes she is watching him.

MIRANDA

Alas, now, pray you,
Work not so hard: I would the lightning had
Burnt up those logs that you are enjoined to pile!
Pray, set it down, and rest you: when this burns,
'Twill weep for having wearied you. My father
Is hard at study; pray, now, rest yourself;
He's safe for these three hours.

FERDINAND

O most dear mistress,
The sun will set before I shall discharge
What I must strive to do.

MIRANDA

If you'll sit down,
I'll bear your logs the while: pray, give me that;
I'll carry it to the pile.

FERDINAND

No, precious creature,
I had rather crack my sinews, break my back,
Than you should such dishonor undergo,
While I sit lazy by.

MIRANDA

It would become me
As well as it does you; and I should do it
With much more ease; for my good will is to it,
And yours it is against. You look wearily.

FERDINAND

No, noble mistress; 'tis fresh morning with me
When you are by at night. I do beseech you,—
Chiefly that I might set it in my prayers,—
What is your name?

MIRANDA

        Miranda. —O my father,
I have broke your hest to say so!

FERDINAND

                Admired Miranda!
Indeed the top of admiration! worth
What's dearest to the world! Full many a lady
I have eyed with best regard, and many a time
The harmony of their tongues hath into bondage
Brought my too diligent ear: for several virtues
Have I liked several women; never any
With so full soul, but some defect in her
Did quarrel with the noblest grace she owed,
And put it to the foil: but you, O you,
So perfect and so peerless, are created
Of every creature's best!

MIRANDA

          I do not know
One of my sex; no woman's face remember,
Save, from my glass, mine own; nor have I seen
More that I may call men than you, good friend,
And my dear father: how features are abroad,
I am skilless of; but, by my modesty,
The jewel in my dower, I would not wish
Any companion in the world but you;
Nor can imagination form a shape,
Besides yourself, to like of. But I prattle
Something too wildly, and my father's precepts
I therein do forget.

FERDINAND

I am, in my condition,
A prince, Miranda; I do think, a king;
I would, not so!—and would no more endure
This wooden slavery than to suffer
The flesh-fly blow my mouth. Hear my soul speak:
The very instant that I saw you, did
My heart fly to your service; there resides,
To make me slave to it; and for your sake
Am I this patient log-man.

MIRANDA

Do you love me?

FERDINAND

O heaven, O earth, bear witness to this sound,
And crown what I profess with kind event
If I speak true! if hollowly, invert
What best is boded me to mischief! I,
Beyond all limit of what else i' the world,
Do love, prize, honor you.

MIRANDA

I am a fool
To weep at what I am glad of.

FERDINAND

Wherefore weep you?

MIRANDA

At mine unworthiness, that dare not offer
What I desire to give; and much less take
What I shall die to want. But this is trifling;
And all the more it seeks to hide itself,
The bigger bulk it shows. Hence, bashful cunning!
And prompt me, plain and holy innocence!
I am your wife, if you will marry me;

FERDINAND AND MIRANDA

If not, I'll die your maid; to be your fellow
You may deny me; but I'll be your servant,
Whether you will or no.

FERDINAND
                    My mistress, dearest;
And I thus humble ever.

MIRANDA
                    My husband, then?

FERDINAND
Aye, with a heart as willing
As bondage e'er of freedom: here's my hand.

MIRANDA
And mine, with my heart in't.

As Miranda finishes speaking, Ferdinand curves his hand around hers so that they stand almost in an attitude of prayer. Then they lean toward each other over their clasped hands and exchange a kiss. The lights dim briefly to indicate the end of the scene.

SHE *removes the pearl chain that had been placed around her neck during the scene and returns it to the box. She takes out instead a parti-colored scarf, shot with bright metallic threads. She does this with a whip-like motion, so that the scarf catches the light sharply as it flares out in the air.*

HE: And now for the bitterness of love, in a scene that is like an opal in the shifting of its moods. We give you a self-tormenting woman who cannot accept love freely. She is Cressida. *(He indicates her.)*

SHE *(indicating him)*: I took Troilus, prince of Troy, as my lover, and I meant to be faithful to him.

HE: And yet the name of Cressida became a byword for un-faithfulness in love.

SHE: How deep is the chasm between what we are and what we would like to be!

HE (*formally, to the audience*): We give you the scene between the lovers in TROILUS AND CRESSIDA.

They turn their backs to the audience as before, and SHE *pulls the scarf up about her with a feverish movement. As the light changes they stand for a moment fixed and then move into each other's arms.*

Cressida is no sooner in the embrace of Troilus than she breaks away sharply.

TROILUS

What too curious dreg espies my sweet lady in the fountain of our love?

CRESSIDA

More dregs than water, if my fears have eyes.

TROILUS

Fears make devils of cherubins; they never see truly.

CRESSIDA

Blind fear, that seeing reason leads, finds safer foot-ing than blind reason stumbling without fear. To fear the worst oft cures the worse.

TROILUS

O, let my lady apprehend no fear. In all Cupid's pageant there is presented no monster.

CRESSIDA

Nor nothing monstrous neither?

TROILUS

Nothing but our undertakings, when we vow to weep
seas, live in fire, eat rocks, tame tigers, thinking it
harder for our mistress to devise imposition enough
than for us to undergo any difficulty imposed. This
is the monstruosity in love, lady, that the will is infinite and the execution confined, that the desire is
boundless and the act a slave to limit.

CRESSIDA

They say all lovers swear more performance than they
are able, and yet reserve an ability that they never
perform, vowing more than the perfection of ten, and
discharging less than the tenth part of one. They that
have the voice of lions and the act of hares, are they
not monsters?

TROILUS

Are there such? Such are not we. Praise us as we are
tasted, allow us as we prove; our head shall go bare
till merit crown it.

CRESSIDA

Boldness comes to me now, and brings me heart.
Prince Troilus, I have loved you night and day,
For many weary months.

TROILUS

Why was my Cressid then so hard to win?

CRESSIDA

Hard to seem won. But I was won, my lord,
With the first glance that ever—pardon me;
If I confess much, you will play the tyrant.

I love you now; but, 'till now, not so much
But I might master it. In faith, I lie,
My thoughts were like unbridled children, grown
Too headstrong for their mother. See, we fools!
Why have I blabbed? Who shall be true to us,
When we are so unsecret to ourselves?
But, though I loved you well, I wooed you not;
And yet, good faith, I wished myself a man,
Or that we women had men's privilege
Of speaking first. Sweet, bid me hold my tongue;
For in this rapture I shall surely speak
The thing I shall repent. See, see, your silence,
Cunning in dumbness, from my weakness draws
My very soul of counsel! Stop my mouth.

TROILUS

And shall, albeit sweet music issues thence. (*He kisses
her.*)

CRESSIDA

My lord, I do beseech you, pardon me;
'Twas not my purpose thus to beg a kiss.
I am ashamed. O heavens! What have I done?
For this time will I take my leave, my lord.

TROILUS

Your leave, sweet Cressid? What offends you, lady?

CRESSIDA

Sir, mine own company.

TROILUS

You cannot shun yourself.

CRESSIDA

Let me go and try.
I have a kind of self resides with you;

But an unkind self that itself will leave
To be another's fool. I would be gone.
Where is my wit? I know not what I speak.

TROILUS

Well know they what they speak that speak so wisely.

CRESSIDA

Perchance, my lord, I show more craft than love,
And fell so roundly to a large confession
To angle for your thoughts. But you are wise;
Or else you love not; for to be wise and love
Exceeds man's might; that dwells with gods above.

TROILUS

O, that I thought it could be in a woman—
As, if it can, I will presume in you—
To keep her constancy in plight and youth,
Outliving beauty's outward, with a mind
That doth renew swifter than blood decays!
Or that persuasion could but thus convince me,
That my integrity and truth to you
Might be affronted with the match and weight
Of such a winnowed purity in love;
How were I then uplifted! But, alas!
I am as true as truth's simplicity,
And simpler than the infancy of truth.

CRESSIDA

In that I'll war with you.

TROILUS

                    O virtuous fight,
When right with right wars who shall be most right!
True swains in love shall in the world to come
Approve their truths by Troilus. When their rhymes,
Full of protest, of oath and big compare,

TROILUS AND CRESSIDA

Want similes, truth tired with iteration,
'As true as steel, as plantage to the moon,
As sun to day, as turtle to her mate,
As iron to adamant, as earth to the center,'
Yet, after all comparisons of truth,
'As true as Troilus' shall crown up the verse,
And sanctify the numbers.

CRESSIDA
                              Prophet may you be!
If I be false, or swerve a hair from truth,
When time is old or hath forgot itself,
When waterdrops have worn the stones of Troy,
And blind oblivion swallowed cities up,
And mighty states characterless are grated
To dusty nothing, yet let memory,
From false to false, among false maids in love,
Upbraid my falsehood! When they've said 'as false
As air, as water, wind, or sandy earth,
As fox to lamb, or wolf to heifer's calf,
Pard to the hind, or stepdame to her son,'
'Yea,' let them say, to stick the heart of falsehood,
'As false as Cressid.' Say 'Amen.'

TROILUS
Amen.

When the scene is ended, SHE *drops the scarf.*

SHE: And now for the final face of love, love the destroyer, in a scene that is as black as all jewels drowned in night.

HE: I am Othello, Moor of Venice. I have let myself believe that my wife is unfaithful to me, and out of my passion and my jealousy I kill the thing I love.

SHE: I am Desdemona, his innocent wife.

HE (*formally*): The murder scene from OTHELLO.

They move to opposite sides of the platform, go one step down and stand motionless throughout the whole of the scene. The stage becomes dark, except for enough light to show their heads and shoulders.

OTHELLO

It is the cause, it is the cause, my soul.
Let me not name it to you, you chaste stars!
It is the cause. Yet I'll not shed her blood,
Nor scar that whiter skin of hers than snow,
And smooth as monumental alabaster.
Yet she must die, else she'll betray more men.
Put out the light, and then put out the light.
If I quench thee, thou flaming minister,
I can again thy former light restore,
Should I repent me; but once put out thy light,
Thou cunning'st pattern of excelling nature,
I know not where is that Promethean heat
That can thy light relume. When I have plucked the
    rose,
I cannot give it vital growth again;
It needs must wither. I'll smell it on the tree.
O balmy breath, that dost almost persuade
Justice to break her sword! One more, one more!
Be thus when thou art dead, and I will kill thee,
And love thee after. One more, and this the last!
So sweet was ne'er so fatal. I must weep,
But they are cruel tears. This sorrow's heavenly,
It strikes where it doth love. She wakes.

DESDEMONA

Who's there? Othello?

OTHELLO

Aye, Desdemona.

DESDEMONA

Will you come to bed, my lord?

OTHELLO

Have you prayed tonight, Desdemona?

DESDEMONA

Aye, my lord.

OTHELLO

If you bethink yourself of any crime
Unreconciled as yet to heaven and grace,
Solicit for it straight.

DESDEMONA

Alack, my lord, what may you mean by that?

OTHELLO

Well, do it, and be brief; I will walk by.
I would not kill thy unpreparèd spirit.
No, heaven forfend! I would not kill thy soul.

DESDEMONA

Talk you of killing?

OTHELLO

Aye, I do.

DESDEMONA

Then heaven

Have mercy on me!

OTHELLO

Amen, with all my heart!

DESDEMONA

If you say so, I hope you will not kill me.

OTHELLO

Humh!

DESDEMONA

Why I should fear I know not.
Since guiltiness I know not; but yet I feel I fear.

OTHELLO

Think on thy sins.

DESDEMONA

They are loves I bear to you.

OTHELLO

Aye, and for that thou diest.

DESDEMONA

That death's unnatural that kills for loving.
Alas, why gnaw you so your nether lip?
Some bloody passion shakes your very frame.
These are portents; but yet I hope, I hope,
They do not point on me.

OTHELLO

Peace and be still!

DESDEMONA

I will so. What's the matter?

OTHELLO

That handkerchief which I so loved and gave thee
Thou gav'st to Cassio.

DESDEMONA

No, by my life and soul!
Send for the man and ask him.

OTHELLO

                      Sweet soul, take heed,
Take heed of perjury; thou art on thy deathbed.

DESDEMONA

Aye, but not yet to die.

OTHELLO

               Yes, presently.
Therefore confess thee freely of thy sin;
For to deny each article with oath
Cannot remove nor choke the strong conception
That I do groan withal. Thou art to die.

DESDEMONA

Then Lord have mercy on me!

OTHELLO

               I say, amen.

DESDEMONA

And have you mercy too! I never did
Offend you in my life; never loved Cassio
But with such general warranty of heaven
As I might love. I never gave him token.

OTHELLO

By heaven, I saw my handkerchief in's hand!
O perjured woman! thou dost stone my heart,
And mak'st me call what I intend to do
A murder, which I thought a sacrifice.
I saw the handkerchief.

DESDEMONA

              He found it then.
I never gave it him. Send for him hither.
Let him confess a truth.

OTHELLO

OTHELLO

He hath confessed.

DESDEMONA

What, my lord?

OTHELLO

That he hath used thee.

DESDEMONA

How? unlawfully?

OTHELLO

Aye.

DESDEMONA

He will not say so.

OTHELLO

No, his mouth is stopped.

Honest Iago hath ta'en order for't.

DESDEMONA

O, my fear interprets. What, is he dead?

OTHELLO

Had all his hairs been lives, my great revenge

Had stomach for them all.

DESDEMONA

Alas, he is betrayed, and I undone!

OTHELLO

Out, strumpet! Weep'st thou for him to my face?

DESDEMONA

O, banish me, my lord, but kill me not!

OTHELLO

Down, strumpet!

DESDEMONA

Kill me tomorrow; let me live tonight!

OTHELLO

Nay, an you strive,—

DESDEMONA

But half an hour!

OTHELLO

Being done, there is no pause.

DESDEMONA

But while I say one prayer!

OTHELLO

It is too late.

The stage goes completely dark, and THE CURTAIN FALLS

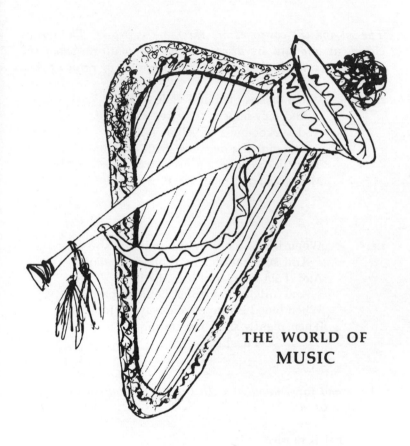

THE WORLD OF
MUSIC

ACT TWO

The set and the costumes are the same as before. The box is closed. HE *and* SHE *are discovered on the platform when the curtain rises, in a tableau that is reminiscent of carol singers.*

SHE: When daisies pied and violets blue
          And lady-smocks all silver-white
       And cuckoo-buds of yellow hue
          Do paint the meadows with delight,
       The cuckoo then, on every tree,
       Mocks married men; for thus sings he,
            Cuckoo,
                Cuckoo . . .

HE: When icicles hang by the wall,
          And Dick the shepherd blows his nail,
       And Tom bears logs into the hall,
          And milk comes frozen home in pail,
       When blood is nipped and ways be foul,
       Then nightly sings the staring owl,
           Tu-whit,
              To-who . . .

They stand for a moment with their heads cocked in a questioning attitude.

SHE: What is music?

HE: We are told it is rhythm and melody—

SHE: That it must use harmony—

HE: Choose tonal color—

SHE: Vary in dynamics and nuance—

HE: And in all this possess form.

There is a pause.

SHE: And *he* tells us that it is a "concord of sweet sounds."

There is another pause. They look out into the space that separates them from the audience.

HE: Where is sound?

SHE: In the speaker?

HE: In the listener?

SHE: Or in the space between?

They have left the platform and reached the forestage. They are now addressing the audience.

HE: Do we not, in this void between us, form an arc for sound?

SHE: Is it not precisely at its center that we exchange, between the voice and the ear, *his* concord?

HE *(in an urgent invitation to the audience)*: Shall we reach?

SHE: Shall we meet?

HE: Listen . . . and we shall place upon the air for you the infinite variety of his music.

SHE *goes to the step on which she stood at the end of the preceding act.*

HE: Listen to his evocation of the beauty of the night. It has the dulcet vibration of a harp.

HE *sits on the steps of the platform, looking up at her.*

SHE: How sweet the moonlight sleeps upon this bank!
    Here will we sit, and let the sounds of music
    Creep in our ears. Soft stillness and the night
    Become the touches of sweet harmony.
    Sit, Jessica. Look how the floor of heaven
    Is thick inlaid with patens of bright gold.
    There's not the smallest orb which thou behold'st
    But in his motion like an angel sings,
    Still quiring to the young-eyed cherubins.

SHE *steps down and* HE *moves to his place on the other side of the platform.*

SHE: Listen again, as a king gathers his soldiers to him on the day of battle. His words have all the bright strength of a trumpet.

SHE *sits on the steps, looking up at him.*

HE: This day is called the feast of Crispian:
    He that outlives this day, and comes safe home,
    Will stand a-tiptoe when this day is named,
    And rouse him at the name of Crispian.
    He that shall live this day, and see old age,
    Will yearly on the vigil feast his neighbors,
    And say, 'Tomorrow is Saint Crispian.'
    Then will he strip his sleeve and show his scars,
    And say, 'These wounds I had on Crispin's day.'
    Old men forget: yet all shall be forgot,

But he'll remember with advantages
What feats he did that day. Then shall our names,
Familiar in his mouth as household words—
Harry the king, Bedford and Exeter,
Warwick and Talbot, Salisbury and Gloucester—
Be in their flowing cups freshly remembered.
This story shall the good man teach his son;
And Crispin Crispian shall ne'er go by,
From this day to the ending of the world,
But we in it shall be rememberèd:
We few, we happy few, we band of brothers;
For he today that sheds his blood with me
Shall be my brother. Be he ne'er so base,
This day shall gentle his condition;
And gentlemen in England, now abed,
Shall think themselves accursed they were not here,
And hold their manhoods cheap whiles any speaks
That fought with us upon Saint Crispin's day.

SHE: There is the reverberation of a drum in the incantation
of the witches in MACBETH.

SHE *joins him on the platform and they act out the spell, using
the box as their cauldron.*

HE: Thrice the brinded cat hath mewed.

SHE: Thrice and once the hedge-pig whined.

HE: Harpier cries, ' 'Tis time, 'tis time.'

SHE: Round about the cauldron go:
           In the poisoned entrails throw.
           Toad, that under cold stone
           Days and nights has thirty-one
           Sweltered venom sleeping got,
           Boil thou first i' th' charmèd pot.

TOGETHER: Double, double, toil and trouble;
Fire burn and cauldron bubble.

HE: Fillet of a fenny snake,
In the cauldron boil and bake;
Eye of newt, and toe of frog,
Wool of bat, and tongue of dog,
Adder's fork, and blind-worm's sting,
Lizard's leg, and howlet's wing;
For a charm of powerful trouble,
Like a hell-broth, boil and bubble.

TOGETHER: Double, double, toil and trouble;
Fire burn and cauldron bubble.

HE: In the same play of MACBETH we have the deep inward note of the horn and the tight percussive insistence of the snare drum.

SHE: Macbeth and his wife are linked in their desire to possess the throne of Scotland and divided in the path they would take.

HE *opens the box and takes out two dark cloaks, which they put on.*

HE: Listen to the interplay of two very different kinds of music as their harmonics blend, clash, rise, fall—chord by chord.

SHE: At this moment Lady Macbeth has just received word that Duncan, king of Scotland, will visit their castle.

HE *moves back into the shadows and stands motionless, his face averted, to indicate that he is not in the scene.* SHE *turns into Lady Macbeth.*

LADY MACBETH

The raven himself is hoarse
That croaks the fatal entrance of Duncan
Under my battlements. Come, you spirits
That tend on mortal thoughts, unsex me here,
And fill me, from the crown to the toe, top-full
Of direst cruelty; make thick my blood,
Stop up th' access and passage to remorse,
That no compunctious visitings of nature
Shake my fell purpose, nor keep peace between
Th' effect and it. Come to my woman's breasts,
And take my milk for gall, you murd'ring ministers,
Wherever in your sightless substances
You wait on nature's mischief. Come, thick night,
And pall thee in the dunnest smoke of hell,
That my keen knife see not the wound it makes,
Nor heaven peep through the blanket of the dark,
To cry, 'Hold, hold!'   *(Enter Macbeth.)*
Great Glamis! worthy Cawdor!
Greater than both, by the all-hail hereafter!
Thy letters have transported me beyond
This ignorant present, and I feel now
The future in the instant.

MACBETH

My dearest love,
Duncan comes here tonight.

LADY MACBETH

And when goes hence?

MACBETH

Tomorrow, as he purposes.

LADY MACBETH

O, never
Shall sun that morrow see!

Your face, my thane, is as a book, where men
May read strange matters. To beguile the time,
Look like the time; bear welcome in your eye,
Your hand, your tongue; look like th' innocent flower,
But be the serpent under't. He that's coming
Must be provided for; and you shall put
This night's great business into my dispatch,
Which shall to all our nights and days to come
Give solely sovereign sway and masterdom.

MACBETH

We will speak further.

LADY MACBETH

                    Only look up clear.
To alter favor, ever is to fear.
Leave all the rest to me.   *(Exit Lady Macbeth.)*

MACBETH

If it were done when 'tis done, then 'twere well
It were done quickly. If th' assassination
Could trammel up the consequence, and catch,
With his surcease, success; that but this blow
Might be the be-all and the end-all here,
But here, upon this bank and shoal of time,
We 'ld jump the life to come. But in these cases,
We still have judgment here, that we but teach
Bloody instructions, which being taught return
To plague the inventor. This even-handed justice
Commends th' ingredients of our poisoned chalice
To our own lips. He's here in double trust:
First, as I am his kinsman, and his subject,
Strong both against the deed; then, as his host,
Who should against his murderer shut the door,
Not bear the knife myself. Besides, this Duncan
Hath borne his faculties so meek, hath been
So clear in his great office, that his virtues

Will plead like angels, trumpet-tongued against
The deep damnation of his taking-off;
And pity, like a naked new-born babe,
Striding the blast, or heaven's cherubin, horsed
Upon the sightless couriers of the air,
Shall blow the horrid deed in every eye,
That tears shall drown the wind. I have no spur
To prick the sides of my intent, but only
Vaulting ambition, which o'erleaps itself,
And falls on th' other—   *(Enter Lady Macbeth.)*
                    How now? What news?

LADY MACBETH

The king's abed.

MACBETH

We will proceed no further in this business.
He hath honored me of late, and I have bought
Golden opinions from all sorts of people,
Which would be worn now in their newest gloss,
Not cast aside so soon.

LADY MACBETH
                    Was the hope drunk,
Wherein you dressed yourself? Hath it slept since?
And wakes it now to look so green and pale,
At what it did so freely? From this time,
Such I account thy love. Art thou afeard
To be the same in thine own act and valor
As thou art in desire? Wouldst thou have that
Which thou esteem'st the ornament of life,
And live a coward in thine own esteem,
Letting 'I dare not' wait upon 'I would,'
Like the poor cat i' th' adage?

MACBETH
                    Prithee peace.

I dare do all that may become a man;
Who dares do more is none.

LADY MACBETH
                              What beast was't then
That made you break this enterprise to me?
When you durst do it, then you were a man;
And, to be more than what you were, you would
Be so much more the man. Nor time nor place
Did then adhere, and yet you would make both.
They have made themselves, and that their fitness now
Does unmake you. I have given suck, and know
How tender 'tis to love the babe that milks me—
I would, while it was smiling in my face,
Have plucked my nipple from his boneless gums,
And dashed the brains out, had I so sworn as you
Have done to this.

MACBETH
If we should fail?

LADY MACBETH
                                We fail.
But screw your courage to the sticking-place,
And we'll not fail. When Duncan is asleep—
Whereto the rather shall his day's hard journey
Soundly invite him—his two chamberlains
Will I with wine and wassail so convince,
That memory, the warder of the brain,
Shall be a fume, and the receipt of reason
A limbeck only; when in swinish sleep
Their drenchèd natures lie as in a death,
What cannot you and I perform upon
Th' unguarded Duncan? what not put upon
His spongy officers, who shall bear the guilt
Of our great quell?

MACBETH AND LADY MACBETH

MACBETH

Bring forth men-children only;
For thy undaunted mettle should compose
Nothing but males. Will it not be received,
When we have marked with blood those sleepy two
Of his own chamber, and used their very daggers,
That they have done't?

LADY MACBETH

Who dares receive it other,
As we shall make our griefs and clamor roar
Upon his death?

MACBETH

I am settled, and bend up
Each corporal agent to this terrible feat.
Away!

*Lady Macbeth moves quickly down the steps to the left part
of the stage and into the darkness. Macbeth looks after her
for a moment as if hypnotized.*

MACBETH

Now o'er the one half-world
Nature seems dead, and wicked dreams abuse
The curtained sleep; witchcraft celebrates
Pale Hecate's offerings; and withered murder,
Alarumed by his sentinel the wolf,
Whose howl's his watch, thus with his stealthy pace,
With Tarquin's ravishing strides, towards his design
Moves like a ghost.

*Lady Macbeth returns and looks at him. Then she moves to
his right and stands waiting. He looks into the shadowed area
from which she has come, and then moves slowly toward it.*

MACBETH

Thou sure and firm-set earth,
Hear not my steps, which way they walk, for fear
The very stones prate of my whereabout,
And take the present horror from the time,
Which now suits with it. Whiles I threat, he lives.
Words to the heat of deeds too cold breath gives.
I go, and it is done.   *(Exit Macbeth.)*

LADY MACBETH

That which hath made them drunk hath made me
    bold.
What hath quenched them hath given me fire.
Hark! Peace!
It was the owl that shrieked, the fatal bellman,
Which gives the stern'st good-night. He is about it.
The doors are open; and the surfeited grooms
Do mock their charge with snores. I have drugged
    their possets,
That death and nature do contend about them,
Whether they live or die.

MACBETH *(within)*

Who's there? What ho!

LADY MACBETH

Alack, I am afraid they have awaked,
And 'tis not done. Th' attempt, and not the deed,
Confounds us. Hark! I laid their daggers ready,
He could not miss 'em. —Had he not resembled
My father as he slept, I had done't. *(Enter Macbeth.)*
My husband!

MACBETH

I have done the deed. Didst thou not hear a noise?

LADY MACBETH
I heard the owl scream and the crickets cry.
Did not you speak?

MACBETH
When?

LADY MACBETH
Now.

MACBETH
As I descended?

LADY MACBETH
Aye.

MACBETH
Hark!
Who lies i' th' second chamber?

LADY MACBETH
Donalbain.

MACBETH *(looking at his hands)*
This is a sorry sight.

LADY MACBETH
A foolish thought, to say a sorry sight.

MACBETH
There's one did laugh in's sleep, and one cried,
    'Murder!'
That they did wake each other. I stood and heard
    them.
But they did say their prayers, and addressed them
Again to sleep.

LADY MACBETH

There are two lodged together.

MACBETH

One cried 'God bless us!' and 'Amen' the other,
As they had seen me with these hangman's hands.
Listening their fear, I could not say 'Amen'
When they did say 'God bless us!'

LADY MACBETH

Consider it not so deeply.

MACBETH

But wherefore could not I pronounce 'Amen'?
I had most need of blessing, and 'Amen'
Stuck in my throat.

LADY MACBETH

These deeds must not be thought
After these ways; so, it will make us mad.

MACBETH

Methought I heard a voice cry 'Sleep no more!
Macbeth does murder sleep'—the innocent sleep,
Sleep that knits up the ravelled sleave of care,
The death of each day's life, sore labor's bath,
Balm of hurt minds, great nature's second course,
Chief nourisher in life's feast,—

LADY MACBETH

What do you mean?

MACBETH

Still it cried 'Sleep no more!' to all the house.
'Glamis hath murdered sleep, and therefore Cawdor
Shall sleep no more. Macbeth shall sleep no more.'

LADY MACBETH

Who was it that thus cried? Why, worthy thane,
You do unbend your noble strength, to think
So brainsickly of things. Go get some water,
And wash this filthy witness from your hand.
Why did you bring these daggers from the place?
They must lie there. Go carry them, and smear
The sleepy grooms with blood.

MACBETH

               I'll go no more.
I am afraid, to think what I have done.
Look on't again I dare not.

LADY MACBETH

               Infirm of purpose!
Give me the daggers. The sleeping and the dead
Are but as pictures. 'Tis the eye of childhood
That fears a painted devil. If he do bleed,
I'll gild the faces of the grooms withal,
For it must seem their guilt.
          (Exit Lady Macbeth. Knock within.)

MACBETH

               Whence is that knocking?
How is't with me, when every noise appalls me?
What hands are here? Ha! They pluck out mine eyes.
Will all great Neptune's ocean wash this blood
Clean from my hand? No. This my hand will rather
The multitudinous seas incarnadine,
Making the green one red.
               (Enter Lady Macbeth.)

LADY MACBETH

My hands are of your color; but I shame
To wear a heart so white. *(Knock.)* I hear a knocking
At the south entry. Retire we to our chamber.

A little water clears us of this deed.
How easy is it then! Your constancy
Hath left you unattended. *(Knock.)* Hark! more
    knocking.
Get on your nightgown, lest occasion call us,
And show us to be watchers. Be not lost
So poorly in your thoughts.

MACBETH

To know my deed, 'twere best not know myself.
    (Knock.)
Wake Duncan with thy knocking! I would thou
    couldst.

*The lights dim to indicate the end of the scene and then come
on full.*

HE: In the vastness of his orchestration no musical color is lost.

SHE: And a favorite sound to his ear was the fool's bell.

HE: Even here he struck every note, from the subtle minor key
of the court fool—

SHE: To the idiotic jingle of the buffoon.

HE: A cheerful sound, and one I very much like.

SHE *(to the audience)*: You too, I think.

HE *(looking at her in hopeful inquiry)*: Shall we?

SHE: You know we must.

*Like released children they rush to the box and come up with
two silly hats.* SHE *also acquires a piece of parchment.*

HE *(to the audience)*: In A MIDSUMMER NIGHT'S DREAM, a group of workmen decide to become actors and present a play. It is a very bad play, but, on the other hand, they are very bad actors.

SHE: The leader of the group is Peter Quince. Or, at least, he is supposed to be the leader.

HE: But a much more important man, at least in his own eyes, is Nick Bottom.

SHE *(putting on one of the comic hats and becoming anxious and willowy)*: Quince has all the effectiveness of a piccolo piping in a high wind.

HE *(putting on the other hat and puffing himself up)*: And Bottom has all the windy self-importance of a very bombastic bassoon.

SHE, *as Quince, unrolls her piece of parchment and looks around at an imaginary gathering of workmen while Bottom stands by helpfully.*

QUINCE
Is all our company here?

BOTTOM
You were best to call them generally, man by man, according to the scrip.

QUINCE
Here is the scroll of every man's name, which is thought fit, through all Athens, to play in our interlude before the duke and the duchess, on his wedding-day at night.

BOTTOM

First, good Peter Quince, say what the play treats on;
then read the names of the actors; and so grow to a
point.

QUINCE

Marry, our play is, The most lamentable comedy,
and most cruel death of Pyramus and Thisby.

BOTTOM

A very good piece of work, I assure you, and a merry.
Now, good Peter Quince, call forth your actors by the
scroll. Masters, spread yourselves.

QUINCE

Answer as I call you. Nick Bottom, the weaver.

BOTTOM

Ready. Name what part I am for, and proceed.

QUINCE

You, Nick Bottom, are set down for Pyramus.

BOTTOM

What is Pyramus? a lover, or a tyrant?

QUINCE

A lover, that kills himself most gallant for love.

BOTTOM

That will ask some tears in the true performing of it:
if I do it, let the audience look to their eyes; I will
move storms, I will condole in some measure. To the
rest: yet my chief humor is for a tyrant: I could play
Ercles rarely, or a part to tear a cat in, to make all
split.

> The raging rocks
> And shivering shocks

> Shall break the locks
>   Of prison-gates;
> And Phibbus' car
> Shall shine from far,
> And make and mar
>   The foolish Fates.

This was lofty! Now, name the rest of the players. This is Ercles' vein, a tyrant's vein; a lover is more condoling.

QUINCE

Francis Flute, the bellows-mender; you must take Thisby on you. It is the lady that Pyramus must love.

BOTTOM

An I may hide my face, let me play Thisby too. I'll speak in a monstrous little voice, 'Thisne, Thisne!' 'Ah Pyramus, my lover dear! thy Thisby dear, and lady dear!'

QUINCE

No, no; you must play Pyramus: and Flute, you Thisby.

BOTTOM

Well, proceed.

QUINCE

Robin Starveling the tailor; you must play Thisby's mother. Tom Snout, the tinker; you, Pyramus' father: myself, Thisby's father: Snug, the joiner; you, the lion's part. You may do it extempore, for it is nothing but roaring.

BOTTOM

Let me play the lion too: I will roar, that I will do any man's heart good to hear me; I will roar, that I

BOTTOM AND QUINCE

will make the duke say, 'Let him roar again, let him roar again.'

QUINCE

An you should do it too terribly, you would fright the duchess and the ladies, that they would shriek; and that were enough to hang us all.

BOTTOM

I will aggravate my voice so, that I will roar you as gently as any sucking dove; I will roar you as 'twere any nightingale.

QUINCE

You can play no part but Pyramus; for Pyramus is a sweet-faced man; a proper man, as one shall see in a summer's day; a most lovely, gentleman-like man: therefore you must needs play Pyramus.

BOTTOM

Well, I will undertake it. What beard were I best to play it in?

QUINCE

Why, what you will.

BOTTOM

I will discharge it in either your straw-color beard, your orange-tawny beard, your purple-in-grain beard, or your French-crown-color beard, your perfect yellow.

QUINCE

Some of your French crowns have no hair at all, and then you will play barefaced. But, masters, here are your parts: and I am to entreat you, request you, and desire you, to con them by tomorrow night; and meet me in the palace wood, a mile without the town, by moonlight. There will we rehearse, for if we meet in the city, we shall be dogged with company, and our devices known. In the meantime I will draw a bill of properties, such as our play wants. I pray you, fail me not.

BOTTOM

We will meet; and there we may rehearse most obscenely and courageously. Take pains; be perfect: adieu.

At the end of the scene they go to the trunk, still holding the hats they have taken off. HE *stands motionless at one side of the box while* SHE *lifts out of it the bearded mask that appeared at the opening of Act I. She faces the audience with the comic hat in one hand and the mask in the other.*

SHE: He was a master of comedy. (SHE *replaces the hat gently.*) Yet he could also create tragedy, heart-shaking and soul-rending. (SHE *holds up the mask.*) We, his instruments, will try to show you one aspect of the mightiest of his plays, KING LEAR.

SHE *turns the mask toward him.* HE *reaches out his hand slowly and there is a moment of ritualistic exchange as he gives her the hat in his hand and accepts the mask instead. His face is intent to the point of exaltation, and again he stands motionless.*

SHE *takes another mask out of the box, one with a woman's face on either side. Then she leaves the platform with the light following her down, so that* HE *is now in darkness.*

SHE *is going to play four parts, those of Lear's three daughters and the Narrator. She now moves into the downstage area that is reserved for the Narrator.*

NARRATOR: The play of KING LEAR has a most complex orchestration. We cannot show you the whole intricate arrangement of the music, but we can indicate the basic motif— the relationship of the King to his three daughters, Cordelia, Goneril, Regan.

As SHE *mentions the last two names, she indicates their faces on the two sides of the mask she is holding.*

King Lear was old, and he decided to divide his kingdom among his three daughters. He called them into his presence, intending to give the most to the one who loved him the best.

The platform lights up to reveal King Lear standing in the center of it, masked and robed and giving an impression of great height.

SHE *leaves the position of the Narrator and moves up one of the steps to play the three daughters, raising the mask to indicate when she is Goneril or Regan, holding it to her side when she is Cordelia.*

LEAR

Meantime we shall express our darker purpose.
Give me the map there. Know that we have divided
In three our kingdom; and 'tis our fast intent
To shake all cares and business from our age,
Conferring them on younger strengths, while we
Unburdened crawl toward death. Tell me, my
        daughters—
Since now we will divest us both of rule,
Interest of territory, cares of state—
Which of you shall we say doth love us most,
That we our largest bounty may extend
Where nature doth with merit challenge. Goneril,
Our eldest-born, speak first.

GONERIL

Sir, I love you more than words can wield the matter,
Dearer than eyesight, space and liberty,
Beyond what can be valued, rich or rare,
No less than life, with grace, health, beauty, honor,
As much as child e'er loved, or father found;
A love that makes breath poor, and speech unable—
Beyond all manner of so much I love you.

LEAR

Of all these bounds, even from this line to this,
With shadowy forests and with champains riched,
With plenteous rivers and wide-skirted meads,
We make thee lady. To thine and Albany's issue
Be this perpetual. What says our second daughter,
Our dearest Regan, wife to Cornwall? Speak.

REGAN

I am made of that self metal as my sister,
And prize me at her worth. In my true heart,
I find she names my very deed of love,
Only she comes too short: that I profess
Myself an enemy to all other joys,
And find I am alone felicitate
In your dear Highness' love.

LEAR

To thee, and thine hereditary ever,
Remain this ample third of our fair kingdom,
No less in space, validity and pleasure,
Than that conferred on Goneril. Now our joy,
Although the last, not least in our dear love.
What can you say to win
A third more opulent than your sisters? Speak.

CORDELIA

Nothing, my lord.

LEAR

Nothing?

CORDELIA

Nothing.

LEAR

Nothing will come of nothing. Speak again.

CORDELIA

Unhappy that I am, I cannot heave
My heart into my mouth. I love your Majesty
According to my bond, no more nor less.

LEAR

How, how, Cordelia! Mend your speech a little,
Lest you may mar your fortunes.

CORDELIA

                              Good my lord,
You have begot me, bred me, loved me. I
Return those duties back as are right fit,
Obey you, love you, and most honor you.
Why have my sisters husbands, if they say
They love you all? Haply, when I shall wed,
That lord whose hand must take my plight shall carry
Half my love with him, half my care and duty.
Sure, I shall never marry like my sisters,
To love my father all.

LEAR

But goes thy heart with this?

CORDELIA

                              Aye, my good lord.

LEAR

So young, and so untender?

CORDELIA

So young, my lord, and true.

LEAR

Let it be so, thy truth then be thy dower.
For, by the sacred radiance of the sun,
The mysteries of Hecate and the night,
By all the operation of the orbs
From whom we do exist and cease to be,
Here I disclaim all my paternal care,
Propinquity and property of blood,
And as a stranger to my heart and me
Hold thee from this for ever. The barbarous Scythian,
Or he that makes his generation messes
To gorge his appetite, shall to my bosom
Be as well neighbored, pitied and relieved,
As thou my sometime daughter.
I loved her most, and thought to set my rest
On her kind nursery.—Hence, and avoid my sight!—

*When Lear has finished speaking he stands motionless until
the next scene begins.* SHE *moves to her corner of the forestage
and again becomes the Narrator.*

NARRATOR: Now that he has cast off Cordelia, Lear plans to
live with his other two daughters in turn, and he goes first
to Goneril. He has brought with him a hundred knights,
and he thinks he can behave as though he were still a
king.

LEAR

How now, daughter, what makes that frontlet on?
You are too much of late i' th' frown.

GONERIL

Not only, sir, this your all-licensed fool
But other of your insolent retinue

Do hourly carp and quarrel, breaking forth
In rank and not-to-be-endurèd riots. Sir,
I had thought, by making this well known unto you,
To have found a safe redress, but now grow fearful,
By what yourself too late have spoke and done,
That you protect this course, and put it on
By your allowance; which if you should, the fault
Would not 'scape censure.

LEAR

Are you our daughter?

GONERIL

Come, sir,
I would you would make use of your good wisdom,
Whereof I know you are fraught, and put away
These dispositions, which of late transform you
From what you rightly are.

LEAR

Does any here know me? This is not Lear.
Who is it that can tell me who I am?
I would learn that; for, by the marks of sovereignty,
knowledge and reason, I should be false persuaded I
had daughters. Your name, fair gentlewoman?

GONERIL

This admiration, sir, is much o' th' savor
Of other your new pranks. I do beseech you
To understand my purposes aright;
As you are old and reverend, should be wise.
Here do you keep a hundred knights and squires,
Men so disordered, so deboshed and bold,
That this our court, infected with their manners,
Shows like a riotous inn; epicurism and lust
Make it more like a tavern or a brothel
Than a graced palace. The shame itself doth speak

For instant remedy. Be then desired
By her, that else will take the thing she begs,
A little to disquantity your train;
And the remainders that shall still depend,
To be such men as may besort your age,
Which know themselves and you.

LEAR

> Darkness and devils!

Saddle my horses; call my train together.
Degenerate bastard, I'll not trouble thee.
Yet have I left a daughter.

GONERIL

You strike my people, and your disordered rabble
Make servants of their betters.

LEAR

Detested kite, thou liest.
My train are men of choice and rarest parts,
That all particulars of duty know,
And in the most exact regard support
The worships of their name. Is't come to this?
Let it be so. I have another daughter,
Who I am sure is kind and comfortable.
When she shall hear this of thee, with her nails
She'll flay thy wolvish visage. Thou shalt find
That I'll resume the shape which thou dost think
I have cast off for ever: thou shalt, I warrant thee.

Lear descends part way down the steps. SHE, *as Regan, comes up behind him and slightly to his left. She is now higher than he is. When Goneril enters the scene,* SHE *moves slightly to his right and assumes Goneril's voice, which is deeper than Regan's as her posture is more erect. The players are almost motionless, with Lear turning his head only slightly from left to right as he speaks to his daughters.*

REGAN

I am glad to see your Highness.

LEAR

Regan, I think you are. Belovèd Regan,
Thy sister's naught. O Regan, she hath tied
Sharp-toothed unkindness, like a vulture, here.
I can scarce speak to thee; thou'lt not believe
Of how depraved a quality—O Regan!

REGAN

I pray you, sir, take patience; I have hope
You less know how to value her desert
Than she to scant her duty.

LEAR

                    Say, how is that?

REGAN

I cannot think my sister in the least
Would fail her obligation. If, sir, perchance
She have restrained the riots of your followers,
'Tis on such ground, and to such wholesome end,
As clears her from all blame.

LEAR

My curses on her!

REGAN

                    O sir, you are old;
Nature in you stands on the very verge
Of her confine. You should be ruled, and led
By some discretion that discerns your state
Better than you yourself. Therefore I pray you
That to our sister you do make return;
Say you have wronged her.

LEAR

Ask her forgiveness?
Do you but mark how this becomes the house:
'Dear daughter, I confess that I am old;
Age is unnecessary. On my knees I beg
That you'll vouchsafe me raiment, bed and food.'

REGAN

Good sir, no more; these are unsightly tricks.
Return you to my sister.

LEAR

Never, Regan.
She hath abated me of half my train,
Looked black upon me, struck me with her tongue
Most serpent-like, upon the very heart.
All the stored vengeances of heaven fall
On her ungrateful top!

REGAN

O the blest gods,
So will you wish on me when the rash mood—

LEAR

No, Regan, thou shalt never have my curse.
Thy tender-hefted nature shall not give
Thee o'er to harshness. Her eyes are fierce, but thine
Do comfort and not burn. 'Tis not in thee
To grudge my pleasures, to cut off my train,
To bandy hasty words. Thou better know'st
The offices of nature, bonds of childhood,
Effects of courtesy, dues of gratitude.
The half o' the kingdom hast thou not forgot
Wherein I thee endowed.

REGAN

Good sir, to th' purpose.—

What trumpet's that?
I know't: my sister's. This approves her letter,
That she would soon be here.

(Enter Goneril.)

LEAR

　　　　　　　　O heavens,
If you do love old men, if your sweet sway
Allow obedience, if you yourselves are old,
Make it your cause. Send down, and take my part.
(To Goneril.) Art not ashamed to look upon this
　　beard?

GONERIL

How have I offended?
All's not offense that indiscretion finds,
And dotage terms so.

LEAR

　　　　　　　O sides, you are too tough.
Will you yet hold?

REGAN

I pray you, father, being weak, seem so.
If, till the expiration of your month,
You will return and sojourn with my sister,
Dismissing half your train, come then to me.

LEAR

Return to her, and fifty men dismissed?
No, rather I abjure all roofs, and choose
To wage against the enmity o' the air,
To be a comrade with the wolf and owl,—
Necessity's sharp pinch! Return with her?
Persuade me rather to be slave and sumpter
To this detested groom.

GONERIL

　　　　　　At your choice, sir.

KING LEAR

LEAR

I prithee, daughter, do not make me mad.
I will not trouble thee, my child; farewell.
We'll no more meet, no more see one another.
But yet thou art my flesh, my blood, my daughter;
Or rather a disease that's in my flesh,
Which I must needs call mine. But I'll not chide thee;
Let shame come when it will, I do not call it;
I do not bid the thunder-bearer shoot,
Nor tell tales of thee to high-judging Jove.
Mend when thou canst, be better at thy leisure;
I can be patient, I can stay with Regan,
I and my hundred knights.

REGAN

Not altogether so;
I looked not for you yet, nor am provided
For your fit welcome. Give ear, sir, to my sister;
For those that mingle reason with your passion
Must be content to think you old, and so—
But she knows what she does.

LEAR

Is this well spoken?

REGAN

I dare avouch it, sir. What, fifty followers?
Is it not well? What should you need of more?
Yea, or so many, sith that both charge and danger
Speak 'gainst so great a number? How in one house
Should many people, under two commands,
Hold amity? 'Tis hard, almost impossible.

GONERIL

Why might not you, my lord, receive attendance
From those that she calls servants, or from mine?

REGAN

Why not, my lord? If then they chanced to slack ye,
We could control them. If you will come to me—
For now I spy a danger—I entreat you
To bring but five and twenty; to no more
Will I give place or notice.

LEAR

I gave you all.

REGAN

And in good time you gave it.

LEAR

Made you my guardians, my depositaries,
But kept a reservation to be followed
With such a number. What, must I come to you
With five and twenty? Regan, said you so?

REGAN

And speak't again, my lord; no more with me.

LEAR

Those wicked creatures yet do look well-favored
When others are more wicked. *(To Goneril.)* I'll go
    with thee;
Thy fifty yet doth double five and twenty,
And thou art twice her love.

GONERIL

Hear me, my lord;
What need you five and twenty? Ten? Or five?
To follow in a house where twice so many
Have a command to tend you?

REGAN

What need one?

LEAR

O, reason not the need. Our basest beggars
Are in the poorest thing superfluous.
Allow not nature more than nature needs,
Man's life is cheap as beast's. Thou art a lady;
If only to go warm were gorgeous,
Why, nature needs not what thou gorgeous wear'st,
Which scarcely keeps thee warm. But for true need,—
You heavens, give me that patience, patience I need!
You see me here, you gods, a poor old man,
As full of grief as age, wretched in both.
If it be you that stirs these daughters' hearts
Against their father, fool me not so much
To bear it tamely; touch me with noble anger,
And let not women's weapons, water-drops,
Stain my man's cheeks. No, you unnatural hags,
I will have such revenges on you both,
That all the world shall—I will do such things;
What they are, yet I know not, but they shall be
The terrors of the earth. You think I'll weep.
No, I'll not weep.
I have full cause of weeping; but this heart
Shall break into a hundred thousand flaws
Or e'er I'll weep.

*Lear descends the rest of the steps and reaches the forestage,
looking up and around as if he had come into the open air.*

LEAR

Blow, winds, and crack your cheeks! Rage, blow!
You cataracts and hurricanoes, spout
Till you have drenched our steeples, drowned the cocks!
You sulphurous and thought-executing fires,
Vaunt-couriers of oak-cleaving thunderbolts,
Singe my white head! And thou, all-shaking thunder,
Strike flat the thick rotundity o' the world,
Crack nature's molds, all germens spill at once

That make ungrateful man.
Rumble thy bellyful! Spit, fire! spout, rain!
Nor rain, wind, thunder, fire, are my daughters;
I tax not you, you elements, with unkindness.
I never gave you kingdom, called you children;
You owe me no subscription. Then let fall
Your horrible pleasure. Here I stand your slave,
A poor, infirm, weak and despised old man.
And yet I call you servile ministers,
That will with two pernicious daughters join
Your high engendered battles 'gainst a head
So old and white as this. O, ho! 'tis foul!

He begins to twist his mantle about him, as if seeking protection.

LEAR

They flattered me like a dog, and told me I had white
hairs in my beard, ere the black ones were there. To
say aye, and no, to everything that I said! Aye, and no
too, was no good divinity. When the rain came to
wet me once, and the wind to make me chatter; when
the thunder would not peace at my bidding; there I
found 'em, there I smelt 'em out. Go to, they are not
men o' their words; they told me I was every thing.
'Tis a lie, I am not ague-proof.

*He tries to get up to the platform again. But he cannot reach
it, and falls brokenly on the steps. There is a long pause and
then Cordelia enters into the light and bends over him
tenderly.*

CORDELIA

O you kind gods,
Cure this great breach in his abusèd nature.
Th' untuned and jarring senses, O wind up
Of this child-changèd father.

O my dear father! Restoration hang
Thy medicine on my lips, and let this kiss
Repair those violent harms that my two sisters
Have in thy reverence made. Alack, alack!
'Tis wonder that thy life and wits at once
Had not concluded all.   (*Lear wakes.*)
How does my royal lord? How fares your Majesty?

LEAR

You do me wrong to take me out o' the grave.
Thou art a soul in bliss, but I am bound
Upon a wheel of fire, that mine own tears
Do scald like molten lead.

CORDELIA
                    Sir, do you know me?

LEAR

You are a spirit, I know. Where did you die?

CORDELIA

Still, still, far wide.

LEAR

Where have I been? Where am I? Fair daylight?
I am mightily abused; I should e'en die with pity,
To see another thus. I know not what to say.
I will not swear these are my hands; let's see—
I feel this pin prick. Would I were assured
Of my condition.

CORDELIA
                    O, look upon me, sir,
And hold your hands in benediction o'er me—
No, sir, you must not kneel.

LEAR
                    Pray, do not mock me.
I am a very foolish fond old man,

Fourscore and upward, not an hour more nor less;
And, to deal plainly,
I fear I am not in my perfect mind.
Methinks I should know you,
Yet I am doubtful. For I am mainly ignorant
What place this is; and all the skill I have
Remembers not these garments; nor I know not
Where I did lodge last night. Do not laugh at me,
For, as I am a man, I think this lady
To be my child Cordelia.

CORDELIA

And so I am—I am.

LEAR

Be your tears wet? Yes, faith. I pray, weep not.
If you have poison for me, I will drink it.
I know you do not love me, for your sisters
Have, as I do remember, done me wrong.
You have some cause, they have not.

CORDELIA

No cause, no cause.
Will't please your Highness walk?

LEAR

You must bear with me.
Pray you now, forget and forgive; I am old and
    foolish.

SHE *leaves the platform and becomes the Narrator.*

NARRATOR: Lear and Cordelia are sent to prison. Yet he is almost happy, since they will be there together.

LEAR

Come, let's away to prison.
We two alone will sing like birds i' the cage.

When thou dost ask me blessing, I'll kneel down,
And ask of thee forgiveness. So we'll live,
And pray, and sing, and tell old tales, and laugh
At gilded butterflies; and hear poor rogues
Talk of court news, and we'll talk with them too,
Who loses, and who wins, who's in, who's out;
And take upon's the mystery of things,
As if we were God's spies. And we'll wear out,
In a walled prison, packs and sects of great ones,
That ebb and flow by the moon.
He that parts us shall bring a brand from heaven,
And fire us hence like foxes. Wipe thine eyes;
The good years shall devour them, flesh and fell,
Ere they shall make us weep. We'll see 'em starve first.
Come.

NARRATOR (*compassionately*): Yet he is denied even that, for
she is murdered in prison before his eyes.

LEAR

Howl, howl, howl! O, you are men of stones.
Had I your tongues and eyes, I'ld use them so
That heaven's vault should crack. She's gone for ever!
I know when one is dead and when one lives;
She's dead as earth.
I might have saved her; now she's gone for ever!
Cordelia, Cordelia, stay a little. Ha!
Why should a dog, a horse, a rat, have life,
And thou no breath at all? Thou'lt come no more,
Never, never, never, never, never.

*Lear turns into a figure as rigid and motionless as stone, and
the light fades into total darkness. When it goes on again,* HE
is still robed but has taken off his mask.

SHE: And now, to end our show, we will give you an entirely

different kind of music, the foot-stamping, hip-swaying, tambourine-tapping rhythm of the dance. We present to you that lively and tempestuous pair, Petruchio and Katharina, in THE TAMING OF THE SHREW.

HE *has already returned his robe and mask to the box. They rummage about in it vigorously, so that* SHE *can deck herself in a scarlet overskirt and he can don a sash and take out a plumed hat. Then he turns to the audience.*

HE: I am Petruchio, and I have come to Padua to get me a rich wife. I have heard that Katharina has a tiger's temper, but I have also heard that she is rich.

HE *puts his hat on his head and turns into Petruchio.*

PETRUCHIO

I will attend her here,
And woo her with some spirit when she comes.
Say that she rail, why then I'll tell her plain,
She sings as sweetly as a nightingale.
Say that she frown, I'll say she looks as clear
As morning roses newly washed with dew.
Say she be mute, and will not speak a word,
Then I'll commend her volubility,
And say she uttereth piercing eloquence.
If she do bid me pack, I'll give her thanks,
As though she bid me stay by her a week.
If she deny to wed, I'll crave the day
When I shall ask the banns, and when be married.
But here she comes; and now, Petruchio, speak.
Good morrow, Kate, for that's your name, I hear.

KATHARINA

Well have you heard, but something hard of hearing;
They call me Katharine that do talk of me.

PETRUCHIO

You lie, in faith, for you are called plain Kate,
And bonny Kate, and sometimes Kate the curst.
But Kate, the prettiest Kate in Christendom,
Kate of Kate-Hall, my super-dainty Kate,
For dainties are all Kates, and therefore, Kate,
Take this of me, Kate of my consolation—
Hearing thy mildness praised in every town,
Thy virtues spoke of, and thy beauty sounded,
Myself am moved to woo thee for my wife.

KATHARINA

Moved? In good time. Let him that moved you hither
Remove you hence; I knew you at the first
You were a moveable.

PETRUCHIO
                          Why, what's a moveable?

KATHARINA

A joint-stool.

PETRUCHIO
                    Thou hast hit it. Come, sit on me.

KATHARINA

Asses are made to bear, and so are you.

PETRUCHIO

Women are made to bear, and so are you.

KATHARINA

No such jade as you, if me you mean.

PETRUCHIO

Alas, good Kate, I will not burden thee.
For, knowing thee to be but young and light,—

KATHARINA

Too light for such a swain as you to catch,
And yet as heavy as my weight should be.

PETRUCHIO

Should be? Should—buzz!

KATHARINA

Well ta'en, and like a buzzard.

PETRUCHIO

Come, come, you wasp, i' faith, you are too angry.

KATHARINA

If I be waspish, best beware my sting.

PETRUCHIO

My remedy is then to pluck it out.

KATHARINA

Aye, if the fool could find it where it lies.

PETRUCHIO

Who knows not where a wasp does wear his sting?
In his tail.

KATHARINA

In his tongue.

PETRUCHIO

Whose tongue?

KATHARINA

Yours, if you talk of tales, and so farewell.

PETRUCHIO

What, with my tongue in your tail? Nay, come again.
Good Kate, I am a gentleman.

KATHARINA
That I'll try.
(She strikes him.)

PETRUCHIO
I swear I'll cuff you, if you strike again.

KATHARINA
So may you lose your arms.
If you strike me, you are no gentleman;
And if no gentleman, why then no arms.

PETRUCHIO
A herald, Kate? O, put me in thy books.

KATHARINA
What is your crest, a coxcomb?

PETRUCHIO
A combless cock, so Kate will be my hen.

KATHARINA
No cock of mine; you crow too like a craven.

PETRUCHIO
Nay, come, Kate, come; you must not look so sour.

KATHARINA
It is my fashion when I see a crab.

PETRUCHIO
Why, here's no crab, and therefore look not sour.

KATHARINA
There is, there is.

PETRUCHIO
Then show it me.

PETRUCHIO AND KATHARINA

KATHARINA

Had I a glass, I would.

PETRUCHIO

What, you mean my face?

KATHARINA

Well aimed of such a young one.

PETRUCHIO

Now, by Saint George, I am too young for you.

KATHARINA

Yet you are withered.

PETRUCHIO

'Tis with cares.

KATHARINA

I care not.

PETRUCHIO

Nay, hear you, Kate. In sooth you 'scape not so.

KATHARINA

I chafe you if I tarry. Let me go.

PETRUCHIO

No, not a whit; I find you passing gentle.
'Twas told me you were rough, and coy, and sullen,
And now I find report a very liar.
For thou art pleasant, gamesome, passing courteous,
But slow of speech, yet sweet as spring-time flowers.
Thou canst not frown, thou canst not look askance,
Nor bite the lip, as angry wenches will;
Nor hast thou pleasure to be cross in talk.
But thou with mildness entertainst thy wooers,
With gentle conference, soft, and affable.

KATHARINA

Where did you study all this goodly speech?

PETRUCHIO

It is extempore, from my mother-wit.

KATHARINA

A witty mother, witless else her son.

PETRUCHIO

Am I not wise?

KATHARINA

Yes, keep you warm.

PETRUCHIO

Marry, so I mean, sweet Katharine, in thy bed.
And therefore, setting all this chat aside,
Thus in plain terms—your father hath consented
That you shall be my wife; your dowry 'greed on;
And will you, nill you, I will marry you.
Now, Kate, I am a husband for your turn,
For by this light, whereby I see thy beauty,
Thy beauty that does make me like thee well,
Thou must be married to no man but me.
For I am he am born to tame you, Kate,
And bring you from a wild Kate to a Kate
Conformable as other household Kates.
                        Never make denial;
I must and will have Katharine to my wife.
And to conclude, we 'greed so well together,
That upon Sunday is the wedding-day.

KATHARINA

I'll see thee hanged on Sunday first.

PETRUCHIO

I tell you, 'tis incredible to believe
How much she loves me.
Give me thy hand, Kate. I will unto Venice,
To buy apparel 'gainst the wedding-day.
I will be sure my Katharine shall be fine.
We will have rings, and things, and fine array;
And kiss me, Kate, we will be married o' Sunday.

*Petruchio slings Katharina over his shoulder, spins her around,
and then sets her brusquely down. She holds the awkward,
puppet-like stance in which she has landed while he moves to
the center of the stage and addresses the audience.*

PETRUCHIO

Thus have I politicly begun my reign,
And 'tis my hope to end successfully.
She ate no meat today, nor none shall eat.
Last night she slept not, nor tonight she shall not.
As with the meat, some undeservèd fault
I'll find about the making of the bed;
And here I'll fling the pillow, there the bolster,
This way the coverlet, another way the sheets.
Aye, and amid this hurly I intend
That all is done in reverent care of her;
And, in conclusion, she shall watch all night,
And if she chance to nod, I'll rail and brawl,
And with the clamor keep her still awake.
This is a way to kill a wife with kindness,
And thus I'll curb her mad and headstrong humor.
He that knows better how to tame a shrew,
Now let him speak, 'tis charity to shew.

*She turns around, looks up forlornly, and straightens in comic
weariness. Then she also comes to the center to address the
audience.*

KATHARINA

The more my wrong, the more his spite appears.
What, did he marry me to famish me?
Beggars, that come unto my father's door,
Upon entreaty have a present alms;
If not, elsewhere they meet with charity.
But I, who never knew how to entreat,
Nor never needed that I should entreat,
Am starved for meat, giddy for lack of sleep,
With oaths kept waking, and with brawling fed;
And that which spites me more than all these wants,
He does it under name of perfect love.

PETRUCHIO

Good Lord, how bright and goodly shines the moon!

KATHARINA

The moon? The sun. It is not moonlight now.

PETRUCHIO

I say it is the moon that shines so bright.

KATHARINA

I know it is the sun that shines so bright.

PETRUCHIO

Now, by my mother's son, and that's myself,
It shall be moon, or star, or what I list,
Or ere I journey to your father's house.
Evermore crossed and crossed, nothing but crossed.

KATHARINA

Forward, I pray, since we have come so far,
And be it moon, or sun, or what you please,
An if you please to call it a rush-candle,
Henceforth I vow it shall be so for me.

PETRUCHIO
I say it is the moon.

KATHARINA
I know it is the moon.

PETRUCHIO
Nay, then you lie. It is the blessèd sun.

KATHARINA
Then, God be blessed, it is the blessèd sun.
But sun it is not, when you say it is not,
And the moon changes even as your mind.
What you will have it named, even that it is,
And so it shall be still for Katharine.

PETRUCHIO
Why, there's a wench! Come on, and kiss me, Kate.

KATHARINA
What, in the midst of the street?

PETRUCHIO
What, art thou ashamed of me?

KATHARINA
No, sir, God forbid; but ashamed to kiss.

PETRUCHIO
Why, then let's home again.

KATHARINA
Nay, I will give thee a kiss.

*She closes her eyes and stands expectantly, waiting for him to
come to her. He stands grandly, waiting for her to come to
him. Finally she opens her eyes, looks at him irresolutely, and*

then begins to move toward him. He does not stir an inch.
She stands on tiptoe and places a gingerly but not unwilling
kiss on his lips.

KATHARINA
Now pray thee, love, stay.

PETRUCHIO
Is not this well? Come, my sweet Kate,
Better once than never, for never too late.

He lifts her exuberantly into his arms and takes her up to the
platform, setting her down very gallantly. He makes a sweep-
ing bow to the audience, and she a curtsey. Then they open
the box and place gently in it the last of their actors' equip-
ment, closing the lid almost with reluctance.

HE: And that's what it's like to be an actor.

SHE: To be everyone—

HE: To feel everything—

SHE: To live many lives—

HE: In many worlds. *(A pause.)*

SHE: The worlds he made for us.

HE: The worlds of William Shakespeare.

They look about them. Then with a slow movement of his
hand in mid-air, HE *brings down the light on the right fore-*
stage as SHE *does the same for the left. The only light remain-*
ing now is on them and their box.

*They sit down on the box, holding hands and smiling at each
other. Then they simultaneously draw down the remaining
light until it turns to darkness and they disappear.*

THE CURTAIN FALLS